EVANGELICALS ON THE CANTERBURY TRAIL

Why Evangelicals Are Attracted to the Liturgical Church

REVISED EDITION

ROBERT WEBBER & LESTER RUTH

MP Morehouse Publishing
NEW YORK · HARRISBURG · DENVER

Morehouse Publishing, 4775 Linglestown Road, Harrisburg, PA 17112

Morehouse Publishing, 445 Fifth Avenue, New York, NY 10016

Morehouse Publishing is an imprint of Church Publishing Incorporated.

www.churchpublishing.org

Cover design by Laurie Klein Westhafer

Typeset by Rose Desgin

Library of Congress Cataloging-in-Publication Data

Webber, Robert.
 Evangelicals on the Canterbury Trail : why evangelicals are attracted to the liturgical church / Robert E. Webber ; revised by Lester Ruth.—[Rev. ed.].
    p. cm.
  ISBN 978-0-8192-2851-2 (pbk.)—ISBN 978-0-8192-2852-9 (ebook) 1. Evangelicalism and liturgical churches. 2. Anglican converts. 3. Episcopal Church–Membership. 4. Anglican Communion–Membership. I. Ruth, Lester, 1959– II. Title.
 BR1640.W42 2012
 270.8'2–dc23

                                    2012034422

CONTENTS

PART 1
Why the Anglican Tradition?—Robert Webber

PART 2
Other Pilgrims Share Their Stories

PART 3
The Canterbury Trail and Today's Churches

PREFACE TO THE REVISED EDITION
Lester Ruth

Although Robert Webber told it with a touch of sadness toward the end of the original *Evangelicals on the Canterbury Trail*, the story of how a colleague once asked him "Can any good thing come out of Wheaton?" now causes me to smile just a tad. And perhaps it should for anyone who knew Webber and has some idea of the breadth of his impact on worship renewal over the last several decades. Can any good thing come out of Wheaton College (Webber's institution at the time)? Indeed, it definitely can, has, and will, thanks to Bob Webber.

Writing just after the fifth anniversary of his death in April 2007, I can state from personal experience that he is still doing quite a bit of good. His impact continues among those who are influenced today by the wisdom of the ancient church's life. I have the privilege of hearing about this twice a year as I help orient the new students coming into the Institute for Worship Studies, an institution that now bears his name. Asked how it was they ended up enrolling, time and again the students—from Pentecostal to Anglican—affirm it was a certain book, article, or workshop by Bob Webber that opened them to the possibility that paying careful attention to history's treasures is a valid path toward faithfulness and renewal in worship. As John Witvliet of the Calvin Institute of Christian Worship states it, Webber's work has prompted many evangelicals to "take worship seriously" in a way they had not before.

Among his writings, the book you now hold has a particular place of influence. I have heard directly from many of its impact on their own journey onto the Canterbury Trail. I know there are Episcopal and Anglican clergy who took up their vocation because this book stirred them to pick up and head for a new land. Written as Webber's own testimony of his journey from Baptist roots to Anglicanism, and reinforced by others who testified of their similar journey along the trail, this book has served as a kind of guide since 1985 on why such a journey might be desirable and on the delights to be found on it. I offer this revision in the hope it continues the spirit of the original.

The plan for revision was simple: If Robert Webber wrote it, it was kept with only the smallest changes. New are the testimonies of others who have traveled on the Canterbury Trail. These new voices show the gates at the beginning and the end of the trail are still open and inviting. Several new concluding chapters also seek to place these stories in a bit of a broader context, concluding with a revision of the original last chapter as a tribute to Robert Webber as a kind of embodiment of his vision of a holistic church.

There is one other new element: my own word of thanks to those who have made this revision come to pass. Foremost among these are Stephanie Spellers, Nancy Bryan, Jo Bailey Wells, Jessica Jones, Tanner Capps, and especially, Joanne Webber. Thank you, too, to those who have contributed to this revision and to those whose stories inspired me in this process even though I was unable to include them in this edition.

Finally, I encourage readers to be generous in their reading of Webber's original references to the "Episcopal Church." You will see in this book that currently the Canterbury Trail in the United States does not necessarily pass only through the Episcopal Church denomination, as the original version tended to presume. The materials below reflect this variety even though Webber's original term has been retained. More explanation is provided in one of the concluding chapters.

PREFACE TO THE 1985 EDITION
Robert Webber

Recently, when I was giving lectures at an evangelical college, a faculty member asked if we could meet somewhere privately.

When we were seated in the privacy of his office, I could tell by his darting eyes and fidgety mannerisms that he was nervous. Clearing his throat and adjusting his body to a comfortable position, he began. "The reason I wanted to talk with you is that I find myself following a spiritual journey similar to yours. My family and I have been active members of a local evangelical church for a number of years, but find we need something more. We now attend the early service at a local Episcopal church, then go to the church where we are members for Sunday school and morning service. That's okay for now, but we can't go on forever like that. Can you give us some advice?"

Then there is another scenario that happens in my office quite frequently. A student will drop by and say, "Can I talk to you about the liturgical church?" While some are interested in becoming involved in the church, others are only curious.

There are other students who are already involved in liturgical churches. They want to talk about the concern expressed by parents who don't know how to deal with the fact that their child is being drawn to a Christian tradition other than their own.

And when I speak in liturgical churches, there is always a great deal of curiosity about evangelicals. Who are they? How do they differ from fundamentalists? What kind of influence might they have in the liturgical church?

These four groups of people—those who are in a serious spiritual pilgrimage into the liturgical tradition, students and others who may be curious, parents who are bewildered, and liturgical Christians who want clarification about the evangelicals in their midst—are the people to whom this book is written.

Evangelicals on the Canterbury Trail will not answer every question. But it will at least provide an introduction to the phenomenon of evangelicals moving toward the liturgical tradition. While I cannot provide any statistics stating how many people are involved in this movement, I can say that I am overwhelmed by the number of people I meet who are either journeying the pilgrimage described in this book, or at least somewhat influenced by the concern to restore aspects of historic Christianity inadequately represented in their own church.

A book like this cannot be written without the help and influence of many people—friends, teachers, ministers, students, and colleagues. I wish to express special thanks to deaconess Leanne Payne, Father George Monroe, Father James Barr, and Bishop James Montgomery for their help and availability to me during my entrance into the Episcopal Church. A word of appreciation also goes out to the Wheaton College administration and to my colleagues for allowing me to journey into the liturgical experience without accusing me of having abandoned the evangelical tradition. And to the contributors to this book whose names appear with their stories, I give thanks. Finally, I wish to acknowledge the expertise and dedication of my editors Floyd Thatcher and Kathleen Mohr. Because they too have traveled the path to Canterbury, their sensitivity to the subject has gone beyond duty into personal involvement and commitment.

INTRODUCTION

In his introduction to this book's first edition, Harold Lindsell wrote, "the Kingdom of God is broader than any denomination." I wholeheartedly concur. Nonetheless, despite the dangers, potholes, and obstacles common to all church trails, the Canterbury Trail can also lead the traveler to the revelation of God's story in scripture and history.

—Dr. James R. Hart, President,
Robert E. Webber Institute for Worship Studies,
Orange Park, Florida

For most people, Reformation Day, October 31, 1972, was just another day. But for me it was a day, a turning point in my life. About 10:30 that morning I was sitting on a large blue chair in Edman Chapel between the president and the chaplain of Wheaton College, waiting to speak to a crowd of more than two thousand Wheaton students and faculty.

I always get nervous when I speak, and today was no exception. I could feel my hands moisten, my throat go dry, and my stomach tighten as I watched students running, squirming, and twisting while attempting to find their seats.

Many of these students' faces were familiar to me—close friends or students from my classes. Others I didn't recognize. Nevertheless, I felt I knew something about all their happy faces. We were united by a common background. For many of us, family structures, family expectations, and church experiences were similar. It didn't matter whether we came from Maine or California, Minnesota or Florida, the cultural context of our evangelical experiences was as familiar as an old shoe.

I wondered, "What will they think of my sermon today?" But I didn't have much time to think about it because we were called to sing Luther's well-known hymn, "A Mighty Fortress Is Our God." The organ was up and out full tremolo, and the students bellowed out the hymn with great enthusiasm. I watched those faces as we sang. I knew that many of these students were from leading evangelical homes—children of evangelical pastors, college and seminary professors, college presidents, missionaries, leaders of mission agencies, directors of magazine and book publishers, and worldwide leaders.

The hymn ended.

The president prayed the invocation.

I was introduced.

"Today," the president explained, "Bob Webber, a member of the Bible and Religion faculty, is going to speak to us on the glories of the Reformation. The sixteenth century was a great period in church history, and we wait with anticipation to hear of God's good work in that era, a work from which we still benefit today."

"Oh, oh," I said to myself, "that was the wrong thing to say for this speech. The president isn't going to like what I'm going to say."

I stood to my feet, walked with some uncertainty to the pulpit, and began. "The modern historian Jaraslov Pelikan has written of the 'tragic necessity' of the Reformation. As Protestants we have frequently heard talks on the necessity of the Reformation. My guess is, however, that most of us have never heard a talk on the tragedy of the Reformation. On this Reformation Day I wish to speak to you on that forbidden subject—'The Tragedy of the Reformation.'"

The next Sunday I walked into an Episcopal church to stay.

Why would I, the son of a Baptist minister, become an Episcopalian? Why would I, a graduate of Bob Jones University, walk the Canterbury Trail? Why would I, an ordained minister of the Reformed Presbyterian denomination, forsake my orders? Why would I, a professor at a mainline evangelical college, risk misunderstanding and put my career in possible jeopardy to follow my heart?

Why is it that my journey is not an isolated example, but an illustration of a much wider phenomenon within the evangelical community? What is it about the liturgical church that has attracted so many of us through its doors? What conditions within evangelicalism may have created the desire for this journey into a more ancient tradition?

The answers to these questions are not easy. Yet, they must be addressed because a growing number of people are moving out of fundamental and evangelical church groups and into mainline churches. I want to write to those whose hearts are pulling them in this direction and to those who are puzzled or upset over this movement.

Specifically, this book is about my personal journey and that of a number of other people into the Episcopal Church. But the current immigration is not exclusively into that church. Many evangelicals are returning to Presbyterian, Lutheran, Methodist, and other historic denominations as well. Thus, this book is about the movement back into the mainline church in general.

I am well aware that you may have one of several reactions to our pilgrimages. For example, those of you who find your faith within a more recent tradition may have some questions about what you read here. Please keep in mind that I'm not asking you to join us on the same journey. But I'm urging you to try to understand and empathize with those of us who are on the Canterbury Trail. Others of you may find that some of the longings and deep-found desires that have moved us toward Canterbury are needs that you seek to fulfill in your own Christian experience. Even though you may not be headed toward Anglicanism, you may identify with us and try to incorporate some of its practices into your own tradition.

Frankly, I think there is much from the Anglican tradition that can enrich and strengthen the evangelical church. But Christianity is like a diamond. To see it in all of its fullness and beauty, we must see it from all of its sides. Anglicanism has a side to it that is not found within the evangelical church. And the opposite of this is true. Evangelicalism has strengths that can enrich and strengthen the Anglican tradition as well.

So, if you are an Anglican reading this book and thinking, "Aha, finally these evangelicals are seeing the light," please don't become too smug just yet. Or if you are an Anglican saying, "Yikes, an invasion of evangelicals in our midst, who needs that? Not me," I ask you to suspend judgment as you read. You might be pleasantly surprised by our contributions to your church.

Since the Sunday that I entered the Episcopal Church, I have often reflected on my pilgrimage in faith. I have thought not only about the years preceding that Sunday, but the more than a decade that has passed by since then. To help me better understand and describe my journey, I think of it in terms of walking through three stages of faith: *familial faith, searching faith*, and *owned faith*.

Familial Faith

The first seven years of my life were spent in the deep heart of Africa, in the jungles of what was then called Belgian Congo. My parents, who were missionaries in the small village of Mitulu, were committed fundamentalists. Both my mother and father had traveled independently to Africa where they met, married, and worked together to evangelize the natives. My father even took safaris into the jungle to reach the pygmies who had never seen a white person, let alone heard about Christ. Sometimes I would go with him.

There were three of us kids—me, an older sister, and a younger brother. When my brother became seriously ill, my parents decided to return to America, where my father became pastor of the Montgomeryville Baptist Church in Montgomeryville, Pennsylvania, a small town about twenty-five miles west of Philadelphia.

The parsonage adjacent to the church was home, and I was the *preacher's kid*—a constricting label I couldn't escape. I was the kid who couldn't go to the movies, the kid who had to keep Sunday as a holy day (no sports), the kid who had to watch everything I did and said.

But I wasn't just a preacher's kid. I was also a fundamentalist Baptist. From an early age, it was thoroughly ingrained within me that I was both a fundamentalist *and* a Baptist. Being Christian wasn't enough. The best Christians were fundamentalists. And the best fundamentalists were Baptists. Catholics were pagan. Episcopalianism was a social club. Lutherans had departed from the faith. Presbyterians were formalistic. And Pentecostals were off-center. Now I may not have been taught these overly simplistic convictions explicitly. But I must have picked them up somewhere in my youth, because for a long time this is what I believed with all my heart. I'll call this type of belief system *familial faith*.

Searching Faith

I tell my students at Wheaton College that the college years are good years to test familial faith. I ask, "Do you believe what you believe because your parents believe it, or do you believe what you believe because you have looked at the options and you own it?" There is a certain amount of risk to *searching faith*, that transition period when you test your familial faith in order to come into *owned faith*.

During my years as an undergraduate, I was not invited to enter into searching faith. On the contrary, searching faith was taboo. To ask genuine questions, to test the options, to be open to other traditions was seen as a sign of doubt.

For example, I remember a number of times when the college founder, speaking in the chapel, would cup his right hand over his mouth, jerk the upper part of his body backward, look to the ceiling, and cry, "So you want to know where a man stands with God?"

Now everyone wants to know where a man stands with God, so this question always grabbed the attention of the student body. "You only have to ask him one question," he said, replying to his own challenge.

Of course, we sat there with our attention fixed on this dynamic man. "What is that question?" we thought.

Then came the answer, thundering through the auditorium, "What do you think of this university?"

This kind of attitude does not foster intellectual curiosity. Instead, it encourages the perpetuation of a fixed faith through memorization and an institutionalization of thought. But then, we all have a tendency to institutionalize our particular brand of the Christian faith and treat our interpretation of the faith as truth.

At any rate, it was this inflexible spirit that I encountered in college that first sent me into searching faith. I said to myself, "This can't be the one and only interpretation of the faith. How can we cancel out all the godly people of church history and the many other living traditions in which people express their faith? Could it be," I asked, "that God has a mold into which he wants to stamp us all?" Because I couldn't come to that conclusion, I found myself wandering away from that particular fold, leaning toward a more inclusive rather than exclusive view of the faith.

I continued to encounter an exclusivism in faith in the seminaries I attended. It gradually dawned on me that *everybody* holds not only to the faith, but to an interpretation of the faith. As I studied historical theology in graduate school, my eyes became opened to numerous boxes into which God and the faith had been placed. And, as the result of the long-range impact of an ecumenical fellowship that I joined and about which I will tell you later, I gradually became aware that behind all of these various interpretations of the faith is one faith.

Owned Faith

I often tell my students that the history of the Christian faith can be compared to an artichoke. The kernel is found in the very center, hidden by layers of leaves. The layers represent the traditions we have built around the truth, traditions that sometimes stand in the way of encountering the truth in its naked power.

Just as we need to peel off the leaves of an artichoke to get to its heart, so in the Christian faith we need to peel away the layers of tradition that take us to the heart of faith.

My own experience is similar to this. I have come to appreciate all the traditions for what they are. They are not the truth, they are the interpretations, the layers of secondary truth, which we have added to the common core of the faith that comes from the apostles and the primitive church.

The church that I now claim as my own and the one that is owned by the other contributors to this book is a particular tradition, the Anglican tradition. But I think we would all say that Anglicanism itself is not the truth, it is one way of describing and living out the truth of Jesus Christ, living, dying, and rising again for the salvation of the world.

The actual substance of faith, the content that stands behind every Christian tradition, is Jesus Christ. It is the Jesus interpreted by the apostles and summarized in the Apostles' Creed. This is the Christ I believed in as a boy, the one whom I searched to know in a deeper way in all the educational institutions I attended, the one whom I now worship in the liturgical church.

So, my pilgrimage into the Anglican tradition is no repudiation of orthodoxy. Rather, it is the affirmation of six aspects of orthodoxy that were not adequately fulfilled for me in my Christian experience. I'll simply state those reasons here and reserve comment on them until the next section of this book.

For me, Anglicanism preserves in its worship and sacraments the sense of mystery that rationalistic Christianity of either the liberal or evangelical sort seems to deny. I found myself longing for an experience of worship that went beyond either emotionalism or intellectualism. I believe I've found that for myself in the Anglican tradition. I also felt a need for visible and tangible symbols that I could touch, feel, and experience with my senses. This need is met in the reality of Christ presented to me through the sacraments. These three needs—mystery, worship, and sacraments—are closely related.

At times I also felt like an ecclesiastical orphan looking for spiritual parents and a spiritual identity. I am now discovering my spiritual identity with all God's people throughout history, by embracing the church universal and a holistic perspective on spirituality. These three needs—historic identity, an ecclesiastical home, and a holistic spirituality—are also closely related.

In the first section of *Evangelicals on the Canterbury Trail*, I describe my own spiritual journey in these six areas of faith. I'm not sure that one has to become an Anglican to satisfy these longings that I and others like myself have experienced. I know many Christians in other traditions who also experience the inclusive reality of which I write. However, all of us whose stories are included in this book feel the Anglican church is a refuge, a home, a place where an intuitive and inclusive Christianity is taught and practiced.

In the second section, several evangelicals who, like me, have made the trek into the Episcopal Church will tell their stories. Their experiences say something very positive about evangelicalism. For me, evangelicalism is certainly a lot less exclusive than it used to be. It is rapidly developing an inclusive spirit—a spirit in which all Christians who own the core of faith, no matter what their tradition, are acceptable.

Another matter of interest is that the presence of an increasing number of Anglicans in the evangelical movement and evangelicals in the Anglican church may cause ripples of influence to move in both directions. What will the increasing number of Anglican theologians and leaders within evangelical institutions mean for the evangelical church? And what will the presence of evangelicals in local Episcopal churches, seminaries, and various agencies mean for the Episcopal Church? Surely these movements contribute to the breaking down of the walls that have separated us in the past. As you read the stories of these six contributors, mutually penetrating influences will become more apparent.

I hope no one will construe this book as an attack against fundamentalism and evangelicalism. I have high regard for my conservative past, and I know many devout Christian people who find great joy and spiritual fulfillment in this tradition. It is not my intention to deny the validity of their experience.

As I write, I recall an experience I had recently. I was visiting my parents in Mechanicsburg, Pennsylvania. On Sunday night we went to the Independent Baptist Church of Shiremanstown, the church my parents regularly attend.

I watched people file into the church and attempted to catch the spirit of what was happening. The organ was playing favorite evangelical music, such as "Wonderful Grace of Jesus" and other similar upbeat testimonial songs.

As the people took their seats and greeted one another with a handshake, a hug, or a kiss, I felt a tremendous sense of joy among these people of God. A man sitting down the row from me was tapping his foot to the music, and keeping time with his gum-chewing mouth and bouncing head. His frequent repetition of "Amen" and "Praise the Lord" made it obvious that he was worshiping.

I would never think of suggesting that these people become Anglican. Nor do I for one moment think my Anglican expression of the faith is a higher form of spirituality. Yet, it is a fact that many people like me, who have been reared in a fundamentalist or evangelical background, have made a journey into the Episcopal Church or another more mainline tradition.

This book explores the question "Why?" without making unnecessary negative judgments. It attempts to describe the larger phenomenon of crossing over into what may seem to many fundamentalists and evangelicals to be "foreign territory." I hope you will read *Evangelicals on the Canterbury Trail* with an open mind and an understanding heart.

PART
1

Why the Anglican
Tradition?

ROBERT WEBBER

A Return to Mystery

In my former Pentecostalism, we were always waiting for a "move" of the Spirit to interrupt the routine of the service and give it meaning, but here every word, every image, every pause in silence, the very routine itself—ancient and inspired—is fraught with mystery. The entire service whispers a persistent "Come, Holy Spirit."

—*The Rev. Paul Edgerton, Presbyter,*
The Reformed Episcopal Church (ACNA),
Wilson, North Carolina

Earlier I mentioned that I grew up in Central Africa in a little village called Mitulu. The village was actually a small clearing in the middle of the thick and nearly impenetrable forest for which Africa is so well known.

I still have many fond memories of that forest. I remember the huge trees that soared upward into the sky, weaving their branches into each other like fingers. Hanging from the trees were long, thick vines that made great swings in my more sporting moments. Beneath them were thick, deep green brush and seven-foot-tall elephant grass. Sparkling brooks ran through the forest, occasionally interrupted by a tumbling waterfall. And the forest's silence was broken only by the cries of the monkeys, the sounds of many birds, the rushing winds, and gurgling waters. But most of all, I remember the sense of fear that hovered over it all. All who stepped into the jungle were aware of the stalking lions, the man-eating leopards, the crocodiles and poisonous snakes. Yet I was enchanted by its mystery. I felt then, as I do now, the overwhelming power of God's natural creation. There is a feeling of something beyond—a deep and impenetrable mystery that beckons one to enter into its reality by simply experiencing its power.

For the first seven years of my life, I lived in the jungle and knew nothing about Western civilization except what I was told. I had never seen a big city until my family stopped in Shanghai on our way home to America. I was amazed at the huge, tall buildings of that concrete city, the masses of people, the quickly moving taxi cabs, the clatter of the restaurants, and my first sighting of a trolley car. For some reason, however, industrial and technological society has never given me the same feeling of awe and wonder I experienced in the forest. There seems to be something explainable about what man has accomplished in God's creation, while the creation itself remains a mystery.

As I grew up in the Western culture of America and began attending school, the mystery of my childhood was soon replaced by the Western ideal of the explainable. Everything, even religious experience, I learned, was to be subjected to reason, logic, and observation. Claims to mystery, to wonder, and to the experience of things too deep to explain were looked upon as primitive, anti-intellectual, and weak minded.

Rationalistic Christianity

This concern for a rational understanding of the universe spilled over into my religious education, particularly in college and seminary. For example, I still remember my first survey course of the Old Testament. The teacher walked into class carrying a large syllabus that included more than one hundred pages of facts. In his introduction he told us that all we needed to know for his course was in the syllabus. Memorize it! Indeed, the syllabus represented a masterpiece of organized information about the Old Testament. It contained the important names, dates, and events not only in general, but specifically for every book and chapter of the Old Testament. What happened on the third day of Creation? Who was Moses' mother? What was the name of the last judge? How many feet long was Solomon's Temple? How many chapters are there in the book of Psalms? What were the names of the people who helped Nehemiah rebuild the walls of Jerusalem?

I found myself conscientiously making lists and memorizing names, dates, events, and a whole host of seemingly irrelevant data. By the time the course ended, I had memorized a thousand or more facts. But if someone had asked me, "What is the message of the Old Testament?" or "What kind of sensitivity do you now have to Jahweh; to his love, compassion, and election of Israel; to his relationship to the world and to the peoples of the world; to his concern for justice in the land for the poor and the oppressed?"—I would have looked at this person with a blank stare. I didn't learn anything about the message of the Old Testament, about the movement of God in history, nor did I learn how to discern his contemporary presence and power in the world for me and for the peoples of the world. For me, the Bible had become a textbook of facts to be memorized and regurgitated on an irrelevant test.

Much of my seminary education was characterized by the same mentality. Here the concern was not so much for facts, but for proof of Christian convictions. For example, I remember a study of the resurrection in a course on apologetics. The emphasis of this study centered around the arguments—the "answers"—to be offered to those who deny the resurrection. I have no objection to the critical examination of the New Testament resurrection accounts, nor do I object to a critical evaluation of the arguments set forth against the idea of the bodily resurrection of Jesus Christ from the grave. What I do object to is the treatment of the resurrection or other issues of doctrine that turns matters of faith into scientific issues. I found that the scholastic attempt to prove the resurrection as a scientific fact did not increase my faith at all. If anything, it took away the mystery and the power of the resurrection and turned it into a dry fact that had little to do with my personal struggle to live a Christian life. While I could repeat all the reasons why it was important to believe in the resurrection, I could no longer speak of the meaning of the resurrection in my own life. What was once a mystery that empowered my life was now an objective argument tucked away on a shelf in my brain.

I didn't know it at the time, but I was being swept away into evangelical rationalism, into a proof-texting Christianity, into a Christianity based on scientific inquiry. Christianity was no longer a power to be experienced, but a system to be defended. I had left the impenetrable forest and entered the technological city.

My study of the Bible now turned into a defense of its inspired authorship. I remember in particular a course I took on the Pentateuch. I recall my eager anticipation as I entered that course of study. I really wanted to learn more about the message of the first five books of the Old Testament. I knew how important they were to the Jewish faith, how foundational they were to the Jewish and later the Christian view of God, who entered into covenant with his people to redeem them and to form them into his special people. I wanted to be exposed to the works of God for Israel, to come closer to the one who revealed himself as a redeeming and caring God to these people he called out of Egypt. But how disappointed I was in that course! It seemed the teacher's purpose was to defend the Mosaic authorship of these books. Rather than challenge us to experience the power and mystery of the God who began to work in history, he presented us with arguments against those who denied that Moses wrote these books. I still can't read the Old Testament without being upset over the time I wasted in that class reducing the mystery of God as revealed in the Pentateuch to an exercise in intellectual gymnastics.

I experienced the same frustration in my courses on systematic theology. The assumption of these courses was that the Bible is a prepositional revelation of God to the world. It is, as some evangelicals say, the mind of God written. Since God's mind is written in a book, we who have been made in the image of God (especially gifted with a mind) may study God's mind written and reach a fairly comprehensive, but not exhaustive understanding of him. We are the meat eaters—the ones who are to grow in faith and knowledge of God through our intellectualization of Christian doctrine.

But the opposite happened to me. I felt as though I was following after the God on the blackboard, the God in the textbook. My experience was simply this: The more certain I became about my ability to defend God's existence and explain his character, the less real he seemed to me. But I was afraid to admit my feelings to anyone else, and I scarcely acknowledged what was happening in my soul. I was drying up spiritually. The reservoir of God's presence in my life was running low. But forget that. It really didn't matter. I had the answers. And, after all, I had been taught that the answers were what made the difference.

Giving Up Rational Christianity

In 1968 I came to Wheaton College fresh from my doctoral studies. I was full of knowledge, armed with the answers, and anxious to help the students of the late sixties who were feeling the desperation of the Vietnam War, the loss of meaning to life, and the despair of that historical time.

One of the first courses I was asked to teach was a class called Christian Doctrine. Here's my chance, I thought, to give them the goods, to show them how rationally defensible the Christian faith is and how reasonable it is to believe in the Christian system of things.

I had heard an evangelical leader say, "I believe in Christianity because it is the most rational explanation of the universe. Show me another system more rational and I'll embrace that and give up my Christian faith." Of course, that person always went on to say that he had studied all the religions and philosophies of the world, and that he believed there wasn't any view more rational than the Christian faith. So he was always on safe ground when he uttered his challenge. I also thought I could rationally defend the scripture as God's mind written and then proceed to systematize the truth of scripture into my reformed box.

To be honest, I loved the box into which I had placed God. Everything fit together so neatly and nicely. First, I derived a great deal of security from my system. I didn't have an answer to all questions. But I had *the* answer. If a student asked why there was evil in the world, or why the God of the Old Testament seemed to ordain wars, or did the Bible teach double predestination, all I had to do was punch my theological computer and out came *the* answer. It gave me a feeling of power, a sense that I was always on the side of the angels. I had developed a smug complacency about my ability to handle the mysteries of life with a touch of knowledge.

Second, wrapping God up in my neat little system gave me the power of judgment. I remember, when I first started to teach, a local Arminian challenged me to a duel in the classroom. I took to this challenge as one would take to a sport. Great fun, I thought to myself. We met in my classroom and debated the five points of Calvinism. I was certain I had nailed him to the wall with my clear logic and impressive assembly of biblical texts. I was elated, almost jubilant over what I considered to be my victory. My system, I thought, was simply superior to that of anyone else. I could quickly put the Catholics, the dispensationalists, and the charismatics in their place, because I really believed their understanding of the biblical data and use of logic was faulty and dangerous. Any "true" Christian with a knowledge of the Bible and common sense would agree with me. I was convinced of that. Reason alone would eventually force all into conformity with my interpretation.

I think I already felt that my reliance on reason and the attitude it created was pretentious, even outrageous. But, at the time, it was all I really knew. It had been modeled for me by many of my teachers. It was a position held by many evangelical leaders. So who was I to question its validity?

However, early indications of doubt did begin to emerge in my first year of teaching at Wheaton College. I really wanted to reach the students that were turning away from the faith at that critical moment in time. As I talked to them about their faith and attempted to "keep them in the faith," so to speak, I became gradually but increasingly aware that the answers didn't work. They simply weren't buying into my system. Actually, their questions were more basic, more fundamental than the questions I was answering.

I remember one day in class when I was rattling on about the proofs for the existence of God. A student in the back row raised his hand and said, "I think we need to be honest about certain things."

"What do you have in mind?" I asked.

"Well, you seem to believe that God exists."

"Yes, I do."

"I don't."

"You don't!"

"No, I don't. And these proofs for the existence of God simply don't mean anything to me."

I was momentarily startled by his frank admission. After all, this was Wheaton College, the citadel of American evangelicalism. Who would ever think that an atheist or agnostic would be free to roam its halls of learning?

I asked, "Does anyone else agree with Steve?" To my absolute surprise, several other hands slipped into the air. I was astonished, dismayed, and somewhat perplexed to say the least.

I gave the incident some thought over the next several days and decided it was time for me to take a risk. I knew students were very troubled about the meaning of life in general. I sensed that my students were at least honest doubters. They seemed to be genuine students, willing to ask the tough questions and characterized by integrity. I came back to the next class and said, "Okay, tell me what you want to learn. Maybe I'm missing the mark by giving you all this information." I wasn't questioning my information nor my system of thought, I was simply acknowledging that my questions were not necessarily their questions and that the material was therefore irrelevant to many of them.

I was surprised when none of them seemed to have a handle on exactly what they wanted. Finally, some suggested that we discuss contemporary drama and music as a jumping off point for exploring issues of meaning: Who am I? What is the purpose of life? What gives my life meaning and significance?

We turned to issues more fundamental than those that systematic theology generally asks. We began to probe the meaning and mystery of life by tuning into the question of meaning asked by the artists of our generation. Looking in particular at the theater of the absurd and the human loss of meaning depicted in drama, art, and music, we began to search for a more profound and deeper meaning in life. I can't say we came to adequate conclusions, but for me and most of the people in the course, it was a search in faith that eventually led many of us into a deeper encounter with God in Christ through experience. Let me tell you what happened.

In the fall of the next year, 1969, the chaplain asked me to speak in chapel. Since we were close to a new year and most especially to a new decade, I decided it would be appropriate for me to address the question, "Where are we evangelicals going in the 1970s?" As I pondered and meditated on the topic, it fell very naturally into two parts. The first part, I decided, would be an evaluation of contemporary culture—the kinds of attitudes that ruled my students' lives and those of so many of their generation. The second part would be the answer.

Having settled on this two-part approach to my sermon, I began, several weeks in advance, to prepare what I believed would be an important statement that would help give direction to these students. In the first part of my sermon I traced the rise of despair, the loss of meaning, and the current conviction that God was dead. Then I focused on the second part.

"What can we tell a world of despairing people?" I asked. My outline began with the typical answer. We can tell them, I said, that God created the world and that the world is, therefore, characterized by meaning. We can tell them that God created human persons in his own image. We can tell them that humanity fell away from God. We can tell them that

Christ came to redeem people from their sins . . . on and on I went, sharpening up the same old answers, repeating the same propositions, delivering the same message.

As I continued to refine the answers, I asked myself, "Webber, why don't these answers do anything for you?" I wasn't questioning the truth of their content. I simply wanted to know why it was all so cold, so calculated, so rational, so *dead*. But I could come up with no alternative, so I wrote all these typical answers down on a piece of paper.

The night I finished my preparation, which was still several days before the sermon, I laid awake wondering about those answers. Why didn't the answers work? Why didn't they work for my students? For others that I knew? For myself? And how could I, I asked myself, drop these non-answering answers on more than two thousand people when I felt so uneasy about them myself?

The next morning I dragged my tired and weary body, mind, and soul to my office. I sat there at my desk and looked at those yellow, legal-sized pages of notes. I felt comfortable and pleased about the first part of the talk. I sensed that my evaluation of things was a fairly accurate picture of what was going on in the West, in the life of the students, and in my own life. But I said to myself, "Webber, you've got to be honest about those answers. You can't preach that with integrity."

I stretched my arm across the desk, picked up the sermon manuscript, and separated the two parts of the sermon. I put the historical evaluation on my left and the answer on my right. I sat there in silence for a long time just looking at those two parts of the sermon. Then, in a moment of conviction, I stood to my feet, grabbed the answer part of my sermon in both hands, and vigorously crumpled the papers. Raising my right hand and arm high above my head, I tossed those answers with all my power into the wastebasket. I dropped back into my chair and sobbed for several hours. I had thrown away my answers. I had rid myself of a system in which God was comfortably contained. I had lost my security and turned my back on years of defending God's existence, his incarnation, his resurrection, and his coming again.

As I was sitting there in my chair, shed of my pretension and naked before an all-powerful and mighty God, I cried out of the depth of my soul to him. "God," I cried, "where are you? Show yourself to me. Let me know that you are." I was met by an awful silence. But it was not an empty silence. It was the silence of mystery—a silence that closed the door on my answers and broke the system in which I had enslaved God. I wept and I wept.

Shortly after, my student assistant came into my office. I told him what had happened and he wept. I went to my class and told them what had happened and they wept.

The next day I stood before the student body and delivered the first part of my sermon. Then I closed my notebook, looked at them directly, and told them what had happened to me. I told them that the answers don't work, that what we need is not answers about God, but God himself. And I told them how God was more real to me in his silence than he had been in my textbook answers. My God was no longer the God you could put on the blackboard or the God that was contained in a textbook, but a maverick who breaks the boxes we build for him. As a result of that open confession, something happened that I had never experienced before that day, nor have I experienced since. Many students, along with myself, identified the neat little rationalisms we were hanging on to and gave them up for an encounter with the living God. Many of us, though believers, were believers in our personal belief systems, in our cozy sets of answers, in our logical systems about God. We were placing faith in a God-substitute, a creation of our mind, an intellectualized image of God. By giving that up, by throwing it away, we were open to an encounter with God himself—a mystery that defies a complete explanation, a mystery that rises above all rational systems and pat answers. It was a cathartic experience for many of us. As one student said to me, "I felt as though a vacuum had been put in my guts and everything within me was sucked out. I feel clean and whole."

■ ■ ■

If God cannot be contained in a system, where can he be encountered? I didn't know it at the time, but this experience, because it forced me to seek God seeking me, pushed me in the direction of worship and the sacraments. Since neither worship nor the sacraments were given high priority in the local evangelical churches, I had to look elsewhere. My journey into the Episcopal Church and into the mystery of God's saving presence in Christ communicated through worship and the sacraments had begun.

CHAPTER

2

A Longing for the Experience of Worship

The *Book of Common Prayer* has met two deep needs of mine: one for daily prayer and scripture reading, the other for a living connection to the Church through the ages. A touchstone in my stormy passage to adult faith, the Prayer Book still anchors me in Christ-centered worship and directs me in the well-worn paths of Christian discipleship.

—The Rev. Jason Ingalls (Episcopal Diocese of Tennessee), Development Assistant, Ridley Hall, Cambridge, England

I have four teenage children, two girls and two boys. The boys are eighteen and twelve, and the girls are sixteen and fourteen. If you have had any contact with teenagers, you can imagine what it is like in my home. (Webber's children are now grown. Read the story of his daughter, Stefany, below.)

My kids are happy, healthy, normal kids who, like others their age, are crazy about music. The moment they get up in the morning, the radio or stereo is turned on. When the door opens after school, the books are dropped on the coffee table, and a record is automatically dropped on the turntable. And when we get in the car to go someplace, the radio is snapped on before the door is shut.

Now, I happen to like silence. I don't know if it's a reaction to four teenagers or whether the love of silence is simply a part of me. At any rate, when I'm traveling alone in the car, I never listen to the radio. I relish the quiet, the opportunity to be alone with myself and my thoughts.

Recently, however, I was returning from a meeting in Chicago and for some reason or another, I broke my own rule and turned on the radio.

An interview was being conducted with a Harvard psychologist. I didn't get his name, but I quickly tuned into the conversation because he was discussing the issue of meaning in life: What is it that holds our life together and makes life worth living? Apparently the psychologist had published an article or book on the subject.

"I used to argue," he said, "for three important sources of meaning. Now I believe there are four." My ears picked up on this matter. I've always been interested in the quest for meaning, since my own search for meaning was stimulated by the cultural revolution of the sixties.

"In my previous article," the psychologist continued, "I suggested that meaning in life came from a relationship of love, enjoyment of work, and a fulfilling recreational and social life." I began to think about these three very basic aspects of life and listened noddingly as they were discussed. I truly felt I could agree with his assertion. Certainly to love and be loved, to see work as an extension of living and not merely something one does to earn money, and to have a group of family and friends to enjoy life with were all sources of meaning for me.

I reflected on my life and felt there were times when all three of these ingredients were present and working in harmony. But I also remembered this was not always true. There were times when only one part of my life was satisfactory and other times of deep discouragement when it seemed that nothing positive was occurring in any aspect of my life. I recalled how powerful each of these three needs were in my own life. And I sensed the craving within me to be happy and satisfied in my love, my work, and my social life. But I wondered, "What is the fourth?"

Almost on cue the psychologist said, "I now think we must add worship to this list." "Worship," he went on to say, "sets our world in order. It puts God in his proper place and puts us in right relationship to him and everything else."

This statement communicated to my inner being. Indeed, as I looked back over the course of my life for the past ten years, I saw that a motivating factor in my spiritual pilgrimage had been the quest for meaningful worship. I was longing deep down within myself for something more than I had. Something within me was pushing me toward an experience of worship, an encounter with God that was different than the plate being served in the churches where I had been involved.

As I listened to the discussion, I not only agreed with the psychologist, but I was glad I had broken my rule of silence and had listened to the radio. The psychologist helped me put my finger on the reason why I thirsted for worship. According to him, my longing was not unique or unusual. Worship is a basic need shared by all people. A need which, when fulfilled, helps make life more meaningful.

During the past few months, I have interviewed a large number of evangelicals who are on the Canterbury Trail. I always ask, "Why did you choose to walk the Canterbury

Trail?" Without exception, the first reason given to me is, "I wanted to worship God."

It isn't that we don't have worship services in the evangelical world. We do. But some feel that what takes place in those services is not an adequate and personally meaningful experience of worship.

Early Impressions of Worship

My earliest impressions of morning worship revolved around the idea of bringing in the harvest. Members of the congregation, I believed, were expected to bring their unbelieving friends and neighbors to church to expose them to the gospel and put them in a supportive situation that would encourage a personal acceptance of Christ. My experience of worship was an evangelistic model.

During my teenage years, I remember feeling confused when a service ended without a plea to come to Christ, to rededicate one's life, or to heed the call to the mission service. The altar call was the high point of the service. Everything else—the hymns, the scripture, the prayers, and of course the special music—pointed toward the moment of decision.

This approach to morning worship was further supported by my undergraduate experience. During that time, I was told that witnessing and bringing people to Christ were the only reasons for my being and for the existence of the church. I still remember a sermon in which a well-known evangelist claimed that evangelism was the only purpose that made my vocation legitimate. He said, "It's all right for you to be a doctor, as long as you are a soul-winning doctor; it's all right for you to be a lawyer, as long as you are a soul-

winning lawyer; it's all right for you to be a teacher, as long
as you are a soul-winning teacher; it's all right for you to be
a bricklayer, as long as you are a soul-winning bricklayer." I
must have assumed that it was all right to go to worship, as
long as the intent of worship was to win souls.

But I grew weary of listening to preaching and hearing
soul-winning messages. I began to realize that evangelism,
important as it was in the church, could not become a substitute for worship. For me, the straw that broke the camel's back
occurred one summer in 1957 in a church in suburban Philadelphia. A visiting evangelist who had "preached his heart out"
brought us to the final point of the meeting, the invitation. We
sang all the verses of the age-old hymn, "Just As I Am," but no
one stepped forward. After another ten-minute plea, accompanied by threats and tears and all the psychological entice-
ments in the book, we sang the whole hymn again. But there
was no response. With a tone of absolute exasperation in his
voice, the evangelist announced that he was going to count to
ten. After ten, if no one responded, he would wash his hands
of this church and let our blood be on our heads. He counted
to ten, slowly. Then, with the air of an omniscient and all-
powerful judge, he announced that he knew God was working
with someone in that congregation to be saved. But, he went
on to say, "It's too late, the Holy Spirit is gone, the invitation is
finished, the door is closed." I watched this man of God as he
stomped from the pulpit, his face flushed with anger.

I wondered about what he had done and why. I wondered if his anger was related more to his feeling of failure
than to his concern for our eternal welfare. I wondered if
he just wanted another notch on his salvation belt, another

statistic to add to his religious bookkeeping. And I said to myself, "There has got to be more to it than this. What is worship all about anyway?"

My quest led me into an educational approach to worship. The main point of the service, I believed, was to get to the sermon. The sermon was the food that nourished the people, and transformed them. The sermon was, you might say, the main dish of the meal. It was what everyone came for, so it better be good. Whether it was by intent or by design, my seminary education left me with this particular notion of worship. As a student I was told to spend at least half my week preparing for the sermon. It was to be an exegetical sermon, a challenge to the mind and heart.

I must confess that in my days as a preacher, this educational mentality toward worship put me under a terrible strain. I felt that I had to perform intellectually. I felt that my sermons had to be deep, thoughtful, and original or people would simply go to another church. Later as a lay person and churchgoer, a member who came looking for food, this emphasis put me under a different kind of strain. Since I seldom found what I was looking for, I quickly became disenchanted with this kind of worship. It was a vicious circle. I knew there was something wrong about the emphasis on education. But I couldn't break out of it, either as a speaker or a worshiper. All I knew was that preaching as a substitute for worship was not where it was at for me. I didn't realize yet that I had made the church into an educational institution and that what I needed was a worshiping community.

In recent years I have observed other substitutes for worship cropping up in churches and on Christian television. One of them is the entertainment mentality—do something interesting and exciting to draw the crowds! Some of the big churches bring in the Christian superstars to attract the crowds—weightlifters, singers, models, football players . . . you name it. The attitude is that if the guest personalities are well known and Christian, they will attract a larger audience. Then, when the churches have the people's attention, they can sneak in the gospel. Good motive. Poor tactic.

Another substitute is the "possibility" mentality. In this approach to worship, the purpose is to help people recover their self-esteem. We are told, "If they can only discover their own greatness . . . If we can help them tap into their inner resources and put wings on their greatest dreams and ideas, we can help turn their negatives into positives, their clouds into rainbows, their darkness into sunlight." All of this is good. Of course, we want people to feel positive about themselves, to discover their potential, and to fulfill their greatest dreams. But shouldn't we stop for a moment and say, "Hey, what is this thing called worship all about?"

It amazes me that I went through seminary without a course in worship, without any professor asking me to address the question: What is worship all about? That's changing in evangelical seminaries now, but slowly.

My longing for a more satisfying worship grew as each route I took in worship led me to a dead-end street. But after giving up the evangelistic approach to worship and after the unfulfilling experience of educational worship, I didn't know what to do next. I was running out of reasons for being at church. I remember posing the question one day to a group of my friends in an open session on the subject. After dismissing evangelistic, educational, and social reasons for being at church, the only argument we couldn't dismiss was the injunction of Hebrews: "Let us consider how to stir up one another to love and good works, not neglecting to meet together, as is the habit of some" (10:24–25). But what for, we asked? No one in the group really knew, although we all had some vague and pious notions about the need to offer worship to God. But even this, as I think about it now, much later, was something that I was supposed to do. I had replaced the idea of somebody doing something for me—evangelizing me, educating me, entertaining me—with a new focus centering around my feeble efforts to praise God and do something for him. I was thoroughly confused and, frankly, fed up with the confusion.

Two Life-Changing Experiences

In the middle of this quandary, two things happened to me. I visited a Roman Catholic worship service on the Saturday night before Easter, and I began reading about the worship of our early Christian fathers.

I had never heard of the great Easter Vigil, an ancient service that begins on Saturday night and ends with the rising of the sun on Easter Sunday morning. (Most modern churches that still celebrate this service have reduced it to two or three hours.) But in 1972 someone mentioned it to me and urged me to attend. I was tired of singing "Up from the Grave He Arose" and pretending I was excited, so I decided to try something new. I called St. Michael's Catholic Church in Wheaton and found out the time of its Easter Vigil service. I went out of curiosity more than anything else. And I had absolutely no idea what I was getting into.

I opened the door of St. Michael's Church and stepped into the narthex only to discover that I was in total darkness, huddled with about a hundred other people. No one was talking, not even a whisper. As my eyes adjusted to the darkness, I could tell we were standing in a circle around several priests and acolytes. I could smell incense, and through the dim rays of distant light, I could see the outline of the priests holding candles. In the center of the priests there seemed to be a large bowl, but I couldn't tell what it was for. So I stood there in reverent silence with everyone else, waiting for whatever was going to happen.

I didn't have to wait long. All of a sudden the bowl in the center of the group burst into a flash of light and I could see the whole narthex, all the people, and the celebrants. At the same moment a young priest with an operatic voice boomed out in a chant, "The Light of Christ," and everyone began to process into the dark church. The priests went first, holding candles lit from the source of light that was still burning. The priest leading the procession carried a large white candle, at least three feet in height and six inches in circumference. It had the symbol of the cross etched in blue on the side. Later, I learned that this was the paschal candle representing Christ who is the light of the world. The rest of us followed, and we each received a small candle that was lit at the door.

As we moved into the church, our procession stopped three more times while the celebrant chanted, "The Light of Christ." The light, although bright, only cast its lengthening shadows through the sanctuary at first, but, as each of us entered with our candles, the light from the candles increased until it filled the church with its brightness. For the next several hours we listened and responded to scripture readings, we participated in a baptismal service, and the night ended with the celebration of the Eucharist, the great thanksgiving of the church.

I began to feel the resurrection. It was more than evidence that demanded a verdict. It was more than an intellectual proposition proving the empty tomb. I couldn't put my finger on it completely, but I sensed that there was something different, something deeper about this experience of worship than anything else I had been through. I didn't really understand it at the time, but I was experiencing the resurrection. It was no longer a hard cold fact, but a warm reality. I experienced being in the tomb and walking out of that darkness into the marvelous light, the light that conquers evil, the light that is Jesus Christ.

Because this service aroused my curiosity about worship, I turned to sources describing the early Christian worship of the fathers of the church. For these early Christians, worship must have been an event of great joy and festivity. They were celebrating the resurrection of Jesus Christ and feasting in anticipation of his return. In the context of a meal, they read the scripture, related stories about Jesus, interpreted him and his work on the cross in the light of Old Testament prophecy, urged fellow Christians to live lives that were exemplary, and brought food to be distributed to the poor of the community. They also spent time in prayer for their needs, for the needs of others, and like the prayer in the synagogue, they gave thanks to God for his provision. After they had prayed, they took bread and wine, the symbols Christ had given of his broken body and his shed blood, and as Jesus had taught, they remembered him through the celebration of the Eucharist.

I was greatly attracted to the simplicity, the power, and the warmth of this approach to worship. But the church I was attending didn't have such a practice. Since I longed to experience this reality, my family and I left the established church and began a house church modeled after the early Christian communities. About forty other people, mostly married couples from the college, joined us.

Every Sunday we met at our home. We sang, read, and interpreted the scriptures, celebrated Holy Communion, ate a meal together, and spent most of the day in fellowship with each other.

It was an exhilarating spiritual experience at first. But it lasted less than two years because we were a small community of people separated from the larger body of Christ, isolated and alone.

I now view that experience as an important and necessary transition to worship in a more liturgical setting. It was a step toward a public worship that retained the emphasis on the Word and the breaking of the bread within the context of prayer and fellowship.

As I recognized the problems inherent in a house church and, at the same time, grew in my need for a worship that included both the Word and the Eucharist, I began thinking and praying about my next step in faith. It was at this point that my attention turned to the Episcopal Church because it retained the simple structure of worship of the early church.

My initial reaction to the more formal setting in the Episcopal Church was one of confusion and uncertainty. I wasn't used to using a prayer book, responding to scripture, praying spontaneously, singing the Lord's Prayer, saying the creed, kneeling, and receiving communion regularly. I needed to understand better what was going on and what I was doing. So I began to study the meaning of Episcopal worship. Although this is not the place to go into that study in depth, I would like to mention a few things that have helped me appreciate and embrace Episcopal worship.

A Word of Appreciation

First, I am impressed with the fact that worship in the *Book of Common Prayer* is directed toward God. This is evident in the first acclamation of worship: "Blessed be God, Father, Son, and Holy Spirit and blessed be his Kingdom now and forever." I have been put off by the narcissism of much contemporary worship. In this setting the orientation of worship appears to center around me, my feelings, and my experience, rather than around God, his person, and his work in Jesus Christ.

I am reminded of a prayer purportedly written by Hippolytus, a bishop in Rome at the beginning of the third century. In the prayer he says, "Having in memory, therefore, his death and resurrection, we offer to you the bread and the cup, yielding you thanks, because you hast counted us worthy to stand before you and to minister to you."

The idea that worship is a ministry to God, that he loves to be worshiped, and that he made us to worship him dominates the worship of the ancient church. It is early Christian conviction drawn from Revelation 4 and 5. In these chapters, we see the heavenly host gathered around the throne in heaven, singing the praises of the Triune God.

The ancient liturgy named for St. John Chrysostom, a fourth-century bishop from Constantinople, describes worship in this fashion: "We give you thanks also for this ministry (worship and praise); vouchsafe to receive it from our hands, even though thousands of angels and ten thousand of angels stand before you, cherubim and seraphim, with six wings and many eyes, flying on high singing the triumphal hymn proclaiming, crying, and saying: 'Holy, Holy, Holy, Lord of Sabaoth; heaven and earth are full of your glory. Hosanna in the highest. Blessed is he who comes in the name of the Lord. Hosanna in the highest.'" When I worship, I too feel lifted up into the heavenly host. I join them in the praise and worship of Almighty God, Father, Son, and Holy Spirit.

Second, I am impressed with the Christ-centered nature of worship in the *Book of Common Prayer*. The central thrust of worship in the Episcopal tradition, just as it was in the ancient tradition, is to celebrate Jesus Christ as the central cosmic figure of the universe. The prayer of thanksgiving at the Eucharist, for example, is modeled after the vision of the world set forth in scriptures and summarized by Paul in Colossians 1. It recounts creation, the fall, the coming of Jesus in the womb of the virgin, his life, death, burial, resurrection, and coming again as the reason for the great thanksgiving.

Whenever I hear this prayer, I repeat the words silently and allow my imagination to picture everything from the creation to the consummation. The prayer itself and the whole Eucharistic action is a majestic rehearsal of the role Christ has played in creating and recreating the world. During this prayer, I am always moved to give thanks to God for the work of Christ, because I feel the benefit of his death and resurrection is being conveyed to me in a fresh experience of spiritual healing. The mystery of his passion wraps around me, penetrates into my very inner person, cleanses me of my sin, restores my relationship to God, and nourishes me in the faith. Worship has become a kind of evangelistic experience for me, extending the benefits of Christ's death and resurrection to me again and again.

I also appreciate the emphasis on scripture reading in the Episcopal tradition. In the early church, when there were no bibles, the reading of scripture was extensive. In contemporary worship there is much less reading, but the Episcopal Church has retained at least three readings and a psalm. This is more scripture than most churches read on a typical Sunday morning. And, because the lectionary is followed, a central theme pertaining to the season of the church year runs through the scripture lessons. Usually, the sermon is also related to that biblical theme.

For this reason I have found that the worship of the Episcopal Church gives direction to my spiritual life. The scripture readings and theme of the week bring me into a relationship with Christ's life in such a way that I experience the mystery of his passion. During Advent, for example, I am drawn into the mystery of awaiting his coming. Simeon's expression of the anticipation of seeing the Messiah becomes my own longing as my devotion to Christ awaits his birth in Bethlehem.

As I meditate on my worship experience in the Episcopal tradition, I find that I am drawn to it because it is so thoroughly evangelical. I have always confessed Christ as the central person of human history and of my life. Yet, until my worship life was oriented around an ordered experience of Christ not only on a weekly, but on a yearly pattern, I was unable to express in a concrete way my personal commitment to Christ. Weekly worship and the calendar of the sacred year gives direction and definition to my spiritual life. I no longer walk alone as in a lone-ranger Christianity, but I join with millions of Christians around the world in a weekly and yearly devotion that defines our existence in the world.

■ ■ ■

Now the question is: Is there something from this ancient historic tradition of worship that can benefit the evangelical tradition? I think so.

Evangelical worship, for the most part, centers on the preacher. What he says to us, how he says it, and what effect his words have on us appear to be paramount. In seminary the pastor has probably been trained to think that worship centers around him. And years of centering worship around the pastor and his sermon has conditioned the people to expect it and want it. But we have to ask whether or not pastor-centered worship is right and biblical. The evidence of 1 Corinthians 12 and the historical pattern prior to the Reformation era certainly speak against it. And many more people today are becoming increasingly dissatisfied with a pastor-dominated worship experience.

I have discovered that a major reason why people are leaving evangelical churches for Episcopal churches is their longing for a more satisfying experience of worship. Maybe the key to satisfaction within the Evangelical tradition can be found by restoring a worship in which Christ is front center not only in our weekly worship, but in our pattern of yearly personal and corporate worship as well.

A Desire for
Sacramental Reality

Ultimately, it was the deep passion and love for Christ's sacraments that drew me to Anglicanism. I came to realize that they are how Christ gives himself to us. It's deeply human. Spiritual, but also inherently fleshy. My understanding of scripture is key, but the sacraments take center stage in my conversion.

—*A. G. Nelson, Member, St. John's Anglican Church, Stockton, California*

In the fall of 1974, I was deeply concerned about my future church affiliation. I was in a crisis situation. I had already acknowledged to myself that continuation in an independent house church was no longer an option for me. The feeling of isolation from the Body of Christ was becoming more intense, and I needed to make a decision.

I remember walking across campus one sunny afternoon, with my hands in my pockets, my head hanging forward, and my eyes glued to the sidewalk. I was wrestling myself. Who am I spiritually? With whom is my identity? To whom do I belong?

These questions were churning within me when I bumped into Leanne Payne, a charismatic Episcopal deaconess. I knew her fairly well because we had discussed many things together, including the Episcopal Church.

She took one look at me and said, "Bob, what's the matter with you? You look deeply troubled. I see strain in your face and in your eyes."

"You're right," I said and I spilled out my concern over church affiliation.

"Bob," Leanne responded, "let's go to your office and pray."

"Sure," I agreed, without knowing what I was getting into. I assumed she meant to pray like most people pray with each other—bow your head and offer your petition to the Lord.

But Leanne had something else in mind. As we stepped into my office, she said, "Sit down and relax. While you pray quietly, I'm going to lock the door and turn off the light because I don't want anybody walking in on us."

I watched with curiosity as she drew a small silver vial from her pocketbook. She made the sign of the cross over the vial and uttered a brief prayer to set the oil apart as an agent of the Holy Spirit. Then she dipped her thumb into the precious oil and placed that oil on my head in the sign of the cross and in the name of the Father, the Son, and the Holy Spirit.

"Bob," she said, "we are going to do the healing of memories for you and ask God to give you a clear direction in your life." She clasped her hands around the sides of my head and encouraged me to pray through every stage of my spiritual journey. Starting in my pre-school years through high school, college, and seminary, we prayed through my spiritual journey, asking God for a sense of direction. I began to feel a sense of release from the past. To this day the effects of that prayer are still with me. The confusion about my spiritual identity was laid to rest, and my feeling of being drawn into the Episcopal Church was confirmed.

This incident points to the basic sacramental principle: God works through life, through people, and through physical, tangible, and material reality to communicate his healing presence in our lives. The point is that God does not meet us outside of life in an esoteric manner. Rather, he meets us through life incidents, and particularly through the sacraments of the church. Sacrament, then, is a way of encountering the mystery.

A Non-Sacramental Background

I grew up with the view that sacraments were akin to magic. It's not that I knew what the sacraments were. I don't think I could have named them or said anything about their meaning at all. I simply thought of them as part of the liturgy, practiced especially among the Catholics. It was my impression that Catholics looked upon the sacraments as the means to get to heaven. Just get baptized, take the Eucharist, go to confession once in a while, and salvation is guaranteed. If you had asked me whether faith or a spiritual life were part of salvation in the liturgical tradition, I would have said, "No, just take the sacraments and all will be well."

In spite of my superficial view of the sacraments, I did have a strong sense of the importance of baptism and the Lord's Supper in my own experience. My own baptism at age thirteen was not something that was perfunctory. I can still remember the day my father talked to me about my need to be baptized. I was sitting in the kitchen of the Baptist parsonage where we lived, snacking on cookies and drinking a Coke. My father slipped into a chair beside me and said, "Robert, I'm going to be conducting some classes for people who will be baptized this spring. Now that you're thirteen, I think it's time you give serious consideration to the step of baptism. By being baptized you will be making a public confession that you do believe in Christ and that you are willing to follow him." I remember going out on the back porch that night, looking up into the stars, and asking myself whether or not I really believed, whether or not I was willing to take up my cross and follow after Christ. The prospect of my own baptism caused me to choose Christ again in a more intense way, to determine once more to follow him.

I also remember the seriousness with which I received the Lord's Supper. On the first Sunday of every month, we received the bread and wine in a most solemn ceremony. The communion table was always covered with a recently washed and ironed linen cloth, neatly laid over the stack of communion trays. The plates of bread were carefully placed on either side of these trays. Behind the table, there were enough chairs for my father, the pastor, the deacons, and one empty chair symbolizing Christ's presence. The somber sermon, hymns, and prayers almost always focused on the death of Christ. Then before communion was served, it was made clear that everyone should prepare by repenting his or her sins. I can remember how seriously I took this admonition, how I always repented of unknown sins, and how fearful I was of eating and drinking unworthily, damning myself out of a relationship with God.

Allow me to step out of my memory for a moment and comment on my early perceptions of the sacraments. First, as I will expand on later, I had an extremely limited view of the sacraments. I had no sense of how the concept of sacrament—encountering the mystery—could be related to all of life. Even though I frequently encountered God's will for my life in events and through people, I didn't acknowledge my experiences as sacramental. And even though I knew that all of life needed to be related to God, I wasn't aware that I longed for a name to attach to this conviction.

Second, I not only misunderstood the liturgical tradition in regard to baptism and the Lord's Supper, but I even misunderstood my own practice. I thought the liturgical view was that God gave salvation through the sacraments, separate from the faith of the recipient. And I viewed my own practice of baptism and the Lord's Supper as if everything depended on me. On both counts I was wrong. I had failed to recognize that the liturgical tradition calls upon the recipient to have faith, and that, in my Baptist experience, the energy of spiritual fusion with God wasn't coming completely from me. God was really there acting in the baptismal water, and in the bread and wine. In retrospect, I realize I had faith, but I lacked the understanding that God works through tangible and visible means to communicate his healing presence. Nevertheless, my Baptist background prepared me to become sacramental.

Becoming Sacramental

Because of my Baptist background, the words "becoming sacramental" still have an odd ring. And on occasion a red flag goes up in response to such words as liturgical or Eucharist. But these words go back to early Christian vocabulary, and they carry many connotations. Let me try to explain what the idea

of sacrament is and why I find the sacramental dimension of
the church to be a compelling spiritual force in my life.

As we have seen, a primary meaning of sacrament is that
God works through his created order, through visible and
tangible signs. For example, signs like water, bread, wine,
oil, and the laying on of hands are visible and tangible meeting points between God and people. They are the points of
intersection between God's action and human faith. I haven't
always believed this principle. There was a time I would have
tossed this idea out as heretical. I would have insisted that
God always communicates spirit to spirit—his spirit with my
spirit. I would have dismissed any hint of a visible or tangible sign of this meeting as dangerous and non-biblical. But I
changed my mind for two reasons.

First, I've become sacramental because of the incarnation. I've always believed God became human. But not until
ten years ago did I begin to wrestle with the implication of
the incarnation. The incarnation affirms that God became
one of us. He entered into our flesh and blood experience. I
tell my students that the litmus test for orthodoxy is found in
the answer to the following question: "Pinch Jesus, and what
does he say?" The obvious answer is, "Ouch." He was a real
person, just like us, sin excepted.

Now, although I always believed Jesus was human, I never
really thought the idea through. The point, of course, is that
God became present to his world not in a spiritual, bodi-
less, timeless, spaceless way. Rather, he became human in
flesh and blood, in time, space, and history. The incarnation
affirms that God acted through material creation to give us
his salvation. Here then is the sacramental principle again!

God uses his created order as a vehicle of his saving, comforting, and healing presence.

John Calvin, the great Protestant Reformer, captured this sacramental principle rather well when he wrote in the *Christian Institutes* that "our ignorance and slothfulness, and, I may add, the vanity of our minds, require external aids, in order to the production of faith in our hearts, and its increase and progressive advance even to its completion, God has provided such aids." Once I was willing to give up a spiritual spirituality and accept a spirituality rooted in creation and incarnation, in mundane things like water, oil, bread, and wine, as well as in people and incidents, I was on the road to becoming sacramental.

Gaining a better understanding of the early church fathers' use of the word *sacrament* also helped my journey toward becoming sacramental. The word *sacramentum*, I discovered, is a Latin word whose earliest usage means "to make holy." I didn't find that objectionable at all. I began to see that the sacraments, these visible and tangible signs, were means by which my relationship with God in faith was established, repaired, and maintained.

As I read more extensively writers like Tertullian, Irenaeus and Cyprian, Augustine, Ambrose, Athanasius, St. John Chrysostom, and other early church fathers, I became less and less prejudiced. Rather than encountering a pagan idea, I discovered what seemed to me to be a thoroughly evangelical concept of the word.

For example, I was surprised to discover that these fathers thought in terms of one sacrament—one visible, tangible means by which we are brought to God. That means is Jesus Christ. He is *the* sacrament *par excellence.* The fathers never argued for salvation by the sacraments. Rather, the sacraments of water and bread and wine, they said, are the visible, tangible signs of Christ's saving action. The purpose of the sacrament is to signify Christ and thus provide a sign of his encounter with us.

Consequently, the fathers saw many things as sacramental. They recognized many means by which Christ's saving reality was signified. Tertullian, for example, went back to the Old Testament and saw sacramental signs everywhere: the Exodus is sacramental because it points to the Christ event; the offices of prophet, priest, and king are sacramental because they are fulfilled in Christ, who as prophet speaks the Word of God, as priest intercedes for us, and as king rules over his creation. Even the Tabernacle and the Temple, with all their sacrifices and sacred rituals, were seen as sacramental. Surely, the Book of Hebrews interprets the Temple and its religious functions as pointing to Christ and being fulfilled in him. What is important here is that all these visible, tangible, and concrete realities were shadows of what was to come. They looked to Jesus, the person whose reality they signified.

When the early fathers evaluated the New Testament church, they saw that it, like the Old Testament, also contained sacraments, that is, visible signs that take us to Jesus. They spoke not only of baptism and the Lord's Supper as visible means by which we are brought to Christ, but also of the gospels, prayer, the study of doctrine, and the power of a life led as a good example.

I found myself highly attracted to this understanding of the sacraments because it is so Christ centered. But I had to come to grips with the idea that a supernatural Christianity based on "God with us" in Jesus Christ and a sacramental Christianity that recognizes God's continued presence with us in the church through visible signs are really two sides of the same coin. Actually, I discovered that this sacramental sense is not as far removed from my evangelical background as it first appeared. I had always believed the scriptures somehow mysteriously represented the means through which God became present to the reader. All I had to do was extend this principle to all of life and to specific signs of God's acting in the church.

A Sacramental Viewpoint

I have already mentioned that my pilgrimage into the liturgical church was related to my concern for rediscovering mystery. I'm no longer willing to look at my world through the eyes of Enlightenment rationalism. I'm convinced that there is more to life than what can be seen by the naked eye, by literalism, or by reason. A conviction to the supernatural calls me to see what is behind the literal, to penetrate more deeply into the mystery of life.

A sacramental view of life is not much different from a supernatural view of life. It affirms the mystery of the universe and allows that everything in life is, in one way or another, related to the mystery of the Creator and Redeemer. For example, I once saw a poster on which were written the words of a Catholic thinker, Teilhard de Chardin: "Because of creation and even more because of incarnation there is nothing profane for those who know how to see." That's it, I said to myself, that phrase captures the broadest sense of sacrament. Because God created this world and even more because he actually became his creation, creation itself—its material substance, its history, its events, and even my small history within the whole—is not profane or secular. There is a religious underpinning to life, a purpose to everything, an end when all things will work out all right. Therefore, everything in life points to the center, to Christ the Creator and Redeemer in whom all things—visible and invisible—find their meaning. That's sacrament in its broadest sense. As an Evangelical, I already believed this. I simply had not recognized that this was a sacramental view of life. Now I had a name for it.

I also discovered that the idea of sacrament relates to the church. Although all of life is sacred, there is something in life that has the specific function of taking us to Christ, and that is his church. The church is the sign of Christ's redemption; it is the mother of those who would have God as their Father. In the womb of the church we are born to eternal life, and in the arms of the church we are nurtured and carried to safety. So the church, that community of God's people on earth, is sacramental because it takes us to Christ.

And God has given the church specific signs through which he acts to save us, to help us, and to lead us in faith. The two most important signs, clearly taught by Jesus, are baptism and the Eucharist. Baptism is the sign of our entrance into the church, and the Eucharist is the visible reminder that the only way to God is through the broken body and blood of his son Jesus Christ. By receiving the bread and wine, we are continually fed and nourished, for they bring Christ's action on the cross to us again and again. His work is not repeated.

Rather, the application of his work is continually made real as we, in faith, add our "Amen," our "So be it," our "Yes" of acceptance to his recreating and renewing work.

In this view, the sacrament is not a thing in itself, an end, but a means through which Christ encounters us savingly. I'm reminded of a sermon preached by an Episcopal rector at a baptism. He looked the congregation squarely in the eye and said, "I want to remind you, water does not save, only Christ saves. This water," he went on to say, "is the sign of his saving action, the concrete manifestation of his love and acceptance, offered to those who come for baptism."

I find the presence of Christ to be particularly true for me in the sacrament of the Eucharist. When I used to think of it as my personal sign of faith, I always wondered, "Did I take it in the right way? Did I properly prepare myself through the confession of my sins to make myself worthy of the bread and wine? Was my faith strong enough to be pleasing to God? Will his wrath come against me because I wasn't serious enough?" All these worries rolled away when I was set free by understanding that the bread and wine are God's symbols of his love toward me. They now speak to me of the mystery of my salvation. Rather than sending me into myself in search of this or that sin to confess, the Eucharist makes me aware that I never have been and never will be worthy. But more than that, the Eucharist tells me that I am acceptable to God because of Jesus Christ. He has done all that needs to be done to make me acceptable to the Father. This is his sign to me of his work for me. I receive this sign in faith and it effects a healing with God, my neighbor, nature, and me. What Christ did for me on the cross is now extended to me. I receive the benefits of his salvation again and again. So the Eucharist has become the sacrament of my encounter with Jesus Christ. He who saved me at the cross continues to extend his salvation to me through the simple and concrete signs of bread and wine.

The above illustrations remind me of how the early church's approach to the sacraments differed from my earlier views. As I mentioned before, I had looked on the sacraments as my sign of faith directed toward God. My impression was that I could show God that I loved him by being baptized and by eating the bread and drinking the wine. But the early church, and with them the Reformers, presented the sacraments as God's signs, not ours. In and through them God actively conveys himself and his grace. They are his signs, and as I participate in faith, my relationship with him is established, repaired, and maintained.

In history, the church has also identified other specific ways in which God's saving grace in Christ is visibly manifest. These are found in the rites of confirmation, confession, marriage, holy orders, and unction (all of which are technically sacraments in Roman Catholicism). In each of these events, God's grace is present in a very special way to provide assistance in the journey of faith and to meet us in a tangible way.

For example, confirmation is not merely an invention of the medieval church in that its biblical parallel goes all the way back to the reception of the Holy Spirit by the primitive Christian community, described in Acts. Paul, in Ephesians 1:13, makes reference to our "seal by the Holy Spirit." I remember when I knelt before the bishop who placed oil on my forehead and then, clasping his hands on my head, prayed, "Strengthen, O Lord, your servant Robert with your Holy Spirit; empower him for your service, and sustain him all the days of his life. Amen." He then slapped me on the face to remind me that "in this world you will have persecution for Christ's sake." I didn't look at that experience as the moment I received the Holy Spirit. Rather, I looked at it as the sign given by God that the Holy Spirit was given to me.

If I ever doubt God's work of grace for me, my memory of the external act of confirmation is a perpetual reminder that I have been brought into the community of Christ and that I am called to live in the mystery of this relationship with the Triune God and with his people, the church. The fact that this is God's sign to me, rather than my sign to him, in no way detracts from my experience of faith. If anything, it encourages and enriches my faith and trust in God. It brings me to God, to faith in him and his work for me.

I also find confession, now known as the rite of reconciliation, to be thoroughly biblical and evangelical in meaning. Certainly St. John calls us to confession when he says, "If we confess our sins, he is faithful and just, and will forgive our sins and cleanse us from all unrighteousness" (1 John 1:9). In my evangelical background the confession of sin played an important role in my spiritual pilgrimage. I now see the importance of confession through another person. This person, whether a minister, a friend, or a spiritual director, bears the responsibility of holding the confessor accountable.

I have always heard objections to confessing your sins to another person. I've been told that it is much better to go directly to God, because no other person has the power to forgive your sins. This perception of confession contains some misinformation. I remember how I carried fears based on those objections into my first confession, only to have them quickly destroyed.

The purpose of confessing sins to another person has to do with accountability. When we sin, we not only sin against God, but against ourselves and our neighbor. Therefore, it makes sense to confess to God in the sight and hearing of another human who can hold us accountable for our lives. Further, no person himself forgives us. He or she, acting in the name of Christ, simply assures us that when we confess our sins in faith, trusting in God to forgive us, we indeed are forgiven and enter a healing stage. The one to whom we confess is a visible and personal agent of God who proclaims what God promises. In this proclamation we are again reminded of the mystery of redemption: it is God who saves us and heals us and brings us to himself.

Marriage has also been identified as sacramental because it is understood by Paul in the light of the relationship that exists between Christ and the church. Marriage is a concrete situation in which the love that exists between Christ and the church may be exemplified. There is a sacred bond in marriage. It is not merely a human agreement between two people, but an agreement that is to be lived in the context of covenantal commitment. Christ has taken the church to be his bride, to love and cherish as his own body. Marriage is characterized by this kind of commitment. In this day of easy relationships when some turn in a spouse as one would turn in a car, there is a greater need for a truly sacramental concept of an agreement as unique as marriage.

Holy orders or ordination also have come to be acknowledged as sacramental. Here, in this office in which one has been called to do the work of ministry, God's action is being demonstrated. It is, of course, not for everyone. Rather, it is only for those who are called by God to minister in his church. To regard holy orders as sacramental does not deny the priesthood of all believers, a cardinal point of the Reformers. Rather, it affirms that an ordinary member of the church has been given the particular responsibility of handling the Word of God and the administration of the sacraments. In this action the office holder represents Jesus Christ. The old caricature that a priest is a mediator between people and God and therefore denies or usurps the ministry of Christ in the church is not true. In my experience the function of the priest in the Anglican tradition is to be the human representative of God. I find, for example, that a godly priest or minister inspires and motivates me toward holiness. I have experienced a shepherding relationship from the priests of the Anglican tradition. I find that a director of my spiritual life, a person to whom I am accountable for my rule of prayer and Christian life, is helpful in giving me personal spiritual direction.

Another sacrament identified by the church is unction. I've already described my experience with this rite when I recalled the day Leanne Payne prayed with me. My earliest introduction to this rite was related to death. In the medieval church, unction was the sacrament of death rather than the sacrament for wholeness and health. The old view of unction is that it is administered to the dying as they leave this world to assure them of salvation. Since Vatican II, the healing dimension, which is rooted in James 5:12 where the elders are instructed to anoint the sick with oil and pray for them, has been restored.

Recovering a Supernatural Christianity

But why are all these rites important to me? Why do I want something more than the immediate relationship to God established by the new birth? Isn't what I had in the evangelical tradition enough?

I am reminded of a comment made by a minister in the Episcopal Church who was being interviewed for an appointment at St. Barnabas Church in Glen Ellyn. He had been a minister in another Protestant tradition. The question was asked, "Why did you leave your church background to become an Episcopal minister?" I will never forget his answer because it helped me identify one of the aspects of the Episcopal tradition that I found especially helpful in my spiritual journey.

He answered, "I was frustrated as a minister in the free-church tradition because I didn't have adequate tools with which to deal with the problems of my people."

"What, for example?"

"Well, I often visited the sick in hospitals or at home and always felt it was not enough to simply read the scripture and pray with them."

"What else did you want to do?"

"I wanted to offer them a visible and tangible sign of God's power. I wanted to touch them with something real and definite."

"Can you give us an example?"

"Yes, I wanted to be able to take the oil of unction and put it on their heads with the sign of the cross. I think that's a touch from God that adds something to scripture reading and a psalm. But my church frowned on the practice."

I was reminded of my own stay in the hospital when my minister came by and simply prayed for me. I wanted more than that; I wanted to be touched by God and to be left with something specific that conveyed God's action for me in the then and now.

The conversation with the candidate for St. Barnabas also reminded me of a tragic occurrence in the life of one of my former students. This young man graduated from Wheaton College, then from an east coast seminary, and later became a pastor in a small town in Pennsylvania. During the first year of his pastorate, he was diagnosed as having cancer. While in the hospital, he asked the elders of the church where he was pastor to anoint him with oil and pray for him. But they would not because they still believed the old concept that the sacraments and sacramentals were magical. For them, anointing with oil was Catholic and pagan. My friend had to ask the pastor and elders of another church to come and anoint him.

I have found in the past I too was a supernaturalist when it came to the inspiration of the Bible, the deity and resurrection of Jesus, and personal conversion. The practical supernatural dimension of the Christian faith in the sacraments was rejected by me as superstition. I no longer regard the sacraments and sacramentals as magical or pagan. Rather, I have come to believe they are visible means through which the saving and healing action of God through Jesus Christ is communicated to his people. The rites do not save us. They are vehicles through which the salvation of the world accomplished by Christ is extended to us. They bring Christ to us and touch us with his healing power. I am persuaded by my own experience and my study of their use that they provide us with a way to truly touch people with the power of Christ.

■ ■ ■

I do not deny the power of the Holy Spirit working more directly. But I am interested in the fact that our evangelical approach to being born again stands in the tradition of a sacrament. We insist on some external acts that visibly portray the power of Christ to convert the person. When we ask someone to raise his hand for salvation, or stand up and walk the aisle, we are describing a sacramental action.

God communicates to us through visible and tangible means. He came to us in an enfleshed form. He was made man and lived among us. Now he continues to act in our lives through those symbols we call sacraments. I can only testify to the power of that experience as one that continually keeps me in Christ and the church.

CHAPTER

4

The Search
for Spiritual Identity

Looking back, I feel as though I had spent my whole
life pacing over a squeaking floor board, and when I
finally pried it up, I found a lost Van Gogh. Anglicanism was there beneath my feet the whole time. Just
like a work of art, its beauty persuaded me, and
within a short time my primary identity became located
in the story of God and a global, sacramental, and
creedal community.

—*Brandon J. N. Walsh, Student, Duke Divinity School,*
Durham, North Carolina

You will probably remember the celebrated case of Jane
Doe. In 1980, Jane, a blonde woman about thirty-eight
years old who was physically attractive and endowed with a
sound and intelligent mind, turned up in Florida without a
hint of who she was.

I remember reading about her in the papers and
watching her on television, as an all-out nationwide search
was made for her identity. I couldn't fully understand her
dilemma because I have always known who I am. I've always
been claimed by my parents and have a sense of continu-
ity with my past through my friends and my memory of the
schools, events, and people who have shaped my life.

I did, however, allow myself to imagine the frustration that Jane must have experienced, being fully alert to her immediate surroundings but having no recall whatsoever of her parents, childhood, education, work, friends, or anything else in her life.

Jane Doe was a woman in search of an identity. She desperately wanted to know who she was and to whom she belonged.

Although I have never suffered from amnesia in the technical, medical sense, I do think one of the reasons I moved in the direction of the Episcopal Church was my strong desire to find a historical identity. I wanted to belong to church history—to feel myself a part of the past. I wanted to stand in the tradition of those who had gone before me. I felt separated from the past and conscious only of my immediate present. From my conversations with other evangelicals who have moved into the Episcopal Church, I have discovered that my search for a historical identity with the church through the ages is a concern shared by others on the same journey.

The Apostate Church

As far back as I can remember, I was told that the "established" church was apostate. By established church, I don't mean the Catholic or Orthodox church. The apostate nature of these churches was taken for granted. It was my impression that these were pagan perversions of the truth. And it was clear that anyone who was converted from one of those traditions would leave immediately. Staying in the Catholic church was not an option or a matter of discussion. Occasionally, a converted Catholic would speak in church and confirm all these suspicions.

But, for me, the immediate issue of apostasy that was relevant and close at hand had to do with the mainline Protestant church. I was told that it was a clear-cut truth that the Episcopal, Lutheran, Presbyterian, and Methodist churches, to name a few, were beyond hope. They were social clubs filled with liberals, modernists, and apostles of evil. The phrase in Revelation "come out from among them and be ye separate" was applied to the true Christian's relationship to one of these bodies. Real Christians left these centers of abomination.

I still recall the day in the spring of 1945 when two establishment leaders from the American Baptist Convention came to talk with my father, then pastor of the Montgomeryville Baptist Church in Montgomeryville, Pennsylvania. My father, I was told by my mother, was too conservative for the American Baptist Convention. And now, these apostate leaders of the church were putting pressure on my father and other conservatives like him to either change their antiquated views or leave the church.

I sensed that we were martyrs for the truth, that Satan was working through these two ominous-looking men to destroy the truth. I began to feel it was "us" against "them," and I felt proud and confirmed in my Gideon-like complex when my father left the American Baptist Convention and affiliated with the Conservative Baptist denomination.

My sense of standing alone against the tide of doctrinal and spiritual corruption was increased during my undergraduate years. During this time, I was introduced to the "Trail of Blood" theory. True Christians, it was argued, always stood outside the established church. The identity of a modern Christian who was *truly* Christian was with those persons and groups who had been put out of the church, even martyred for the sake of their stand for the faith.

I understood the concept, but still failed to have any identity because no one informed me about these people. Who they were and exactly what they represented remained a mystery to me. I simply knew that to suffer the reproach of being "outside" the main stream of Christianity was somehow the experience of all the true Christians who preceded me.

A Protestant Identity

As I proceeded with my walk through history, I felt that my identity had to be connected somewhere in the Protestant tradition. I wondered if I could find a home with Luther, with Calvin, or with the Anabaptists. I was particularly attracted to John Calvin. I liked his commentaries and his system of thought so clearly laid out in the Institutes. Here was a clear mind, a warm heart, a great leader of the church. I could start with him, I thought.

At the Reformed Episcopal Seminary in Philadelphia, I studied under Robert K. Rudolf, a master teacher and a walking encyclopedia of Calvinist theology. By his magnetic personality and his deep devotion to logically consistent truths, I was soon drawn into the teaching of John Calvin. I thought, "here it is." I swallowed it whole. As I look back on that experience, it was as though I thought God himself had given John Calvin the final, ultimate, complete, and authoritative interpretation of the Bible.

I now had an identity. I belonged, as it were, to the family of Calvinists, that great body of people who referred all questions to the great systematic mind of Calvin. If a question came up, no matter what it was, the method of answering that question was always, "What did Calvin say?" I soon found it was unhealthy to disagree with Calvin or to question his interpretation on any given subject.

I began to suspect that the reason why it was unhealthy to question Calvin was a matter of security. After all, Calvin was not only my ticket to knowing the truth, he was also my means of being able to judge those who didn't agree with me.

My special glee was to put the Arminians down. (Arminius called Calvin's theology into question and began an opposite tradition of interpretation known as Arminianism. This viewpoint is strongly held among the Wesleyan, Pentecostal groups, and the Holiness Tradition in general.) I was also able to distinguish myself from the Lutherans. They were a bit too Catholic, their break from Rome was inadequate. It didn't go far enough. As the Puritans were to say of both Lutherans and Anglicans, they retained "rags of popery." I was also able to set myself against the Anabaptists (Mennonites and Brethren come from them), especially because of their pacifism.

All of this worked very neatly for me, and I felt most comfortable with it until I actually met Arminians, Lutherans, Anabaptists, and Roman Catholics who were devout Christian people. The neat little lines I had drawn to assure my identity were beginning to crumble. The problem as I see it now is that I had gained my identity through an association with a particular historical tradition. I think it would have been appropriate to accuse me of being a Calvinist first and a Christian second. I never would have admitted it, but the fact is that this was true.

My search for an identity took on a whole new perspective in my graduate program. There were two experiences in

particular that stretched me and helped my search for identity to begin to come to closure. Let me tell you about them.

Two Experiences

First of all, I enrolled in a course entitled "The Apostolic
Fathers." I chose the course because it met at a convenient
time and fulfilled a requirement. Little did I know that the
short quarter course would arouse an interest in me, that
now, more than twenty years later, is still not satiated.

The Apostolic Fathers are Christian leaders in the church
who wrote and pastored churches between 100 and 150 A.D.
These include men like Clement, the Bishop of Rome who
wrote a letter to the church at Corinth appropriately called
the first letter of Clement in 96 A.D.; the seven short letters
of Ignatius, Bishop of Antioch who wrote to various churches
en route to Rome where he was to be put to death in the
Colosseum for his faith; and the *Didache*, a short teaching
manual designed to guide early Christian ethical instruction
and practices such as baptism. (There are several others. But
these three influenced me most.)

What was important to me from these writings and writers was not only their thought, but the sense of a *link*—a link
with the apostles. These writers were actually contemporaries
of the apostles, people who grew up at a time when John, for
example, was still living and active in the church. They were
children when some of the New Testament materials like the
gospels were written.

For me, the dawning sense of a link with primitive Christianity was exhilarating. It set in motion a whole new perception for
me, a perception that made me want to march through history

as it happened. I had always looked back on the history of the Church in a judgmental manner. Somehow, I felt that where I was in time and space was *better* than where anyone else had been. Now, because of the link with the apostles, I wanted to stand within history and march forward. I felt like I had found my family tree in the attic. I had this overwhelming urge to discover for the first time my Christian lineage.

Actually, this experience was quite revolutionary. Even though I was in graduate school, I was of the opinion that the church had gone apostate around 100 A.D., at the close of the New Testament age, and wasn't recovered again until the Reformation.

I was of the opinion that apostasy was the order of the day immediately in the church. I know this may appear to be an unintelligent view for someone who had already graduated from seminary. However, at that time evangelical seminaries taught very little church history and placed no emphasis on the church prior to the Reformation. Consequently, my exposure to the church prior to the Reformation was minimal and entirely deficient. For that reason, the myth of an Apostate church from the very beginning was never really addressed. That history, it was assumed, belonged to the Catholics and the Orthodox, and everyone knew that they were questionable expressions of the Christian faith. So, why bother to study people or a movement that was wrong from the start?

The second incident, which happened during my graduate studies in seminary and one which was to have far-reaching implications for my own spiritual pilgrimage, resulted from interest shown in me by one of my teachers, Dr. John Damm. One day after class Professor Damm said,

"Bob, there are a few of us here who are interested in putting together an ecumenical fellowship group. Would you be interested in joining?" "Oh," I said, "that does sound interesting. Who would be involved?" "Well," said John, "myself and a few seminarians from Concordia, a few people from Eden Seminary, and a small handful of Catholic seminarians and priests." I gulped when I heard his last phrase. *A small handful of Catholic seminarians and priests*, I thought. All of a sudden all the images and caricatures of Romanism came to mind. How could I, a dyed-in-the-wool evangelical, a Christian committed to Protestant Christianity, have anything in common with a Roman Catholic? How could we pray together, read and discuss the scripture and fellowship together? Can Jerusalem and Babylon have anything in common?

Dr. Damm raised this question with me in 1965, the year that Vatican II came to an end. Pope John XXIII had opened the windows of the Roman church and had invited fresh winds to blow through the structure. Little did I know that those winds would also blow on me and assist my pilgrimage into an identity with the universal church.

After thinking over the proposal made by my professor, I decided that, threatened as I was by a Catholic presence, it would at least be an interesting experience to have first-hand contact with a few Roman Catholics. My aunt was a Catholic, but it was something that we never discussed in her presence. Other than my aunt, I had never had any personal contact with a Catholic, let alone prayer with a priest. Nevertheless, I decided to grit my spiritual teeth and endure the pain. Maybe, I thought, I could be a witness to these pagans and help them come to a saving knowledge of Christ.

I went to the first meeting with great apprehension and defensiveness. Would these Mary-worshipers, these advocates of works righteousness, these saint-worshipers, and prayers for the dead know anything about true Christianity? Would they be so steeped in tradition, so warped by liturgy, and so attached to their beads that discussion of scripture, personal prayer, and fellowship would be foreign to their experience?

That first evening together was an evening I will never forget. We decided to sit in a circle and share our faith pilgrimages with each other. I still remember one of the seminarians. He was a young blond, short of stature with a boyish face, a disarming grin, and a brilliant mind. I don't remember his name, but I recall that he was a philosophy major, a candidate for a Ph.D. at St. Louis University. He began speaking. "Jesus Christ," he said, "means everything to me. He is my Lord, my Savior, my friend. I want to tell you how I met him." In warm and glowing terms, he shared his faith in Jesus and spoke of his love of the scriptures, his life of prayer, and his concern to get to know Christians from other traditions. His love for Christ and the church was catching, as was the love expressed by the other Catholic seminarians and priests.

As time went on, my prejudices against the Roman Catholics began to fall by the wayside. I had encountered real people who were deeply committed to Christ and his church—people who expressed their faith in a tradition different than mine, but people whom I had to admit challenged me in my own faith experience. I felt that they loved Christ more than I did, that they knew more about the Christian faith than I did, that they cared deeply about prayer and spirituality, and that they were deeply devoted to the poor, the hungry, and the outcasts of this world.

I don't mean to suggest that all Catholics are exactly like these seminarians. But there is one thing I have become convinced of: Evangelical Christians do not have a monopoly on the faith. God has his people in every expression of the faith—Catholic, Orthodox, Protestant, fundamentalist, evangelical, Holiness, charismatic. Christ's saying that "where two or three are gathered together in my name, there am I in the midst" must be understood in a new and radical way in our day of denominationalism and division within the church. He did not say "where two or three are gathered under this particular label (Baptist, Presbyterian, Pentecostal, etc.), there am I in the midst."

Coming Home

My experience of God's people who were of a completely different tradition than mine gave me pause for reflection. "Where," I had to ask myself, "is my identity? Am I an evangelical, a fundamentalist? What am I? Where do I belong?"

I remembered Paul's admonition to the Corinthian church: "For when one says, 'I belong to Paul,' and another, 'I belong to Apollos,' are you not merely men?" (1 Cor. 3:4).

Could it be, I asked, that we need to hear Paul's admonition today in a fresh way? Is the situation in today's church an expanded version of the Corinthian problem? Are we putting our labels before Christ? I was convinced that I had done this and I was resolved to find a way to overcome my failure to affirm the whole church. But I ran into trouble.

I began to declare this newfound sensitivity to the whole church to my classes at seminary and later to my students at Wheaton College. In those days, contrary to today, I found a considerable amount of resistance to my inclusive understanding of the church. Students and colleagues who hadn't shared my experience branded me as a papist, a Protestant going in the wrong direction, a betrayer of the true Protestant tradition. But I was resolved to maintain my convictions, which were born out of experience.

I was also desperate for fellowship with a community of people with whom my experience of a Christian identity, both Catholic and Protestant, was acceptable. I began to toss around the options in my mind. "Where should I go," I wondered. "Could I fit into the Lutheran church? Would I feel more at home in the Episcopal Church?"

In an earlier chapter, I described my encounter with Leanne Payne who prayed for me in my office. For more than an hour, Leanne prayed for me as I brought back to mind the wounds I had received by those who attempted to malign my faith pilgrimage and by those who sought to impede my journey into a wider, more inclusive sense of the Christian faith. After prayer, I felt free, even delivered. What other people thought, what other people said, what other people accused me of doing or believing no longer mattered. What was important for me was to pursue the direction in which I was being led.

Please don't feel that I am urging all others to follow my pilgrimage. I'm only explaining what happened to me. Part of the reason I ended up in the Episcopal Church is that they consciously embraced both Catholic and Protestant traditions. That was more than ten years ago. A lot has happened in the church since then. One thing is the increasing openness to the Catholic tradition among Protestants. Many who would have been condemnatory of my pilgrimage in the early '70s are now much more open and accepting, because old prejudices have been in the process of breaking down in recent years. A new openness toward Protestants on the part of Catholics, and vice versa, has caused us to understand that there is only one church and that the label is secondary. I am a Christian first and an evangelical Episcopalian second.

God saves us not because of the label we wear, but because of what he has done in Jesus Christ for us all. When we truly affirm that confession, then we have found our identity with the history of all God's people. Our family tree begins not with the Reformation or the twentieth-century evangelical movement, but with Jesus Christ, and it continues through the Apostles, the primitive Christian community, the Apostolic Fathers, the Eastern Orthodox church, the Catholic church, the Church of the Reformation, and all who say "Jesus is Lord."

■ ■ ■

To affirm our identity with all God's people everywhere is to recover from historical amnesia and to discover our identity. We belong to a great company of saints. We can claim Augustine, Aquinas, Luther, Calvin, Wesley, and Moody as our ancestors. We belong to them and they to us. Together we are one in Jesus Christ, brothers and sisters in the community of faith with Christ as our head. Thanks be to God!

Embracing the
Whole Church

My experience in Anglicanism has encouraged me to envision a place where both my Pentecostal and Catholic friends can meet under the same roof to celebrate the mystery of the immediate presence of our risen Savior.

—*Matthew Hoppe, Music Pastor, Restoration Anglican Church, Alexandria, Virginia*

In addition to my teaching responsibilities at Wheaton College, I'm also an adjunct professor at Northern Baptist Seminary in Oak Brook, Illinois, a suburb of Chicago. I normally teach one course a year on early and medieval Christianity.

In the spring of 1983, I asked the students of my class to introduce themselves and tell a little about their background and hopes for the future.

One of the first students to speak began by saying, "Well, I grew up in the Catholic church. When I met the Lord, I left and became a Baptist." In this particular course there were at least four or five students out of twenty-two who recited a similar story, so, when it came time for me to give my story, I said, "Well, I grew up in a Baptist background, and when I met the Lord, I became an Episcopalian."

My comment was made tongue-in-cheek and I suspect that the others were as well. While the experience of leaving the Catholic church for these students may have been true, I didn't sense from them a judgmental attitude toward Catholics.

Nevertheless, many Protestants feel the Catholic church is so far removed from the true Christian tradition that those who are in it are not truly Christian. Only recently I was speaking to a Protestant who was telling me about his work in Latin America. As he described the area in which he worked, he said, "Of course there were no Christians there at all, they were all Catholics." I didn't feel it was my place to challenge or embarrass him in the presence of other people. I simply swallowed hard. I realized then and there that the attitude against Catholicism will die hard among Protestants.

But the opposite is true as well. A few years ago I taught a course at the Maryknoll Seminary (Roman Catholic) in Glen Ellyn, Illinois, on contemporary Protestantism. We began the course by swapping stories about our attitudes toward each other. Each of those seminarians confessed that they had grown up with the idea that Protestantism was a heresy, that they should stay away from Protestants, and that the likelihood of Protestants going to heaven was quite slim.

Barriers

Since the days of Vatican II, the barriers between Protestants and Catholics have been breaking down. However, we still have a long way to go before we truly recognize each other. Several recent examples from my own life seem to confirm this.

A few years ago my neighbor, a devout Roman Catholic woman, died. Her children came to me immediately after her death and told me that she had requested before she died that I preach her funeral sermon. Would I do it, I was asked. Of course I would do so, I replied. Shortly after, the priest of the local Catholic church called me to discuss the arrangements. He seemed very nervous and concerned about having a Protestant preach in the Catholic church. He told me that this was unusual, that it was not really allowed, but that since Mrs. Spratt had made the request, he would honor it. And, of course, he reminded me that I could not receive the Eucharist. Although I was aware that I could not receive the Eucharist, it still pained me to be shut out of the communion of those who also affirm Christ as Savior.

I preached on the phrase, "I am the resurrection and the life, he that believeth in me though he were dead, yet shall he live." I spoke of Mrs. Spratt's faith in Christ and her devotion to the church. I affirmed that as Jesus had actually been raised from the dead, so we who believe in him would be raised to everlasting life together with him and all the saints.

The orthodoxy of my sermon apparently caught the priest off guard. He was an older man who probably still had strong misconceptions about Protestants. At the reception he seemed warmer toward me. He thanked me profusely for my sermon and registered surprise at my orthodoxy. I left with a strong feeling of unity and spiritual camaraderie between us.

A similar situation occurred recently in a Russian Orthodox church. Several years ago I taught a course in Eastern Orthodox theology at the Wheaton College summer school session. On one Sunday I scheduled a trip into Chicago to the Orthodox Cathedral, the Church of the Holy Trinity. The people at the church willingly cooperated with me. In addition to letting us attend their service, they appointed a woman who was very knowledgeable about Orthodoxy to meet with us and answer questions.

This woman was talking privately to several of my students. Convinced of her own faith and curious about these students from Wheaton College, she asked them, "Who do you believe Jesus to be?" I suspect she thought they would say something like "a good man who left us an example to live by." Instead they said, "We believe he's the Son of God, who lived and died to redeem the world." The woman was aghast. "You don't say!" she exclaimed. "Why, you're orthodox." She immediately walked over to me and related the incident with a great deal of enthusiasm and amazement. Then, looking me in the eye, she asked, "Do any of these other students believe that?" "Yes," I said, "I can't speak for each one of them, but that certainly is what we believe and teach at Wheaton College." "My stars," she replied, "I didn't think anyone but the Orthodox and Catholics believed that."

I have told you these stories because they illustrate how isolated we are from one another and how suspicious we are of other Christians who are not from our immediate culture and context. Part of my reason for making a pilgrimage into the Episcopal Church is it provides a context in which I can freely affirm the faith of other Christian people without being suspect. Let me share with you more of my background so you can understand why being able to make this broader affirmation of faith is a drawing card to the Episcopal Church.

Separationism

I was first introduced to the theology of separationism while I was in junior high school. My father's experience as a pastor helped create within me the feeling that only those church groups that had left the major denominations were true churches standing in apostolic teaching.

In spite of my background, I wasn't prepared for my introduction into "second-degree separationism," which I first experienced in my undergraduate days.

I'll never forget the day I heard the accusation that "Billy Graham is the greatest tool of the devil in the twentieth century." My mind flashed back to the day in high school when I first heard of Billy Graham. It was right after his Los Angeles crusade, which propelled him into the American limelight. I recalled how I read of him in *Life* magazine and looked at the pictures of his crusade as I sat in the library of the Lansdale High School in Pennsylvania. I remembered how excited I was to realize that someone who preached the gospel could also be accepted and even promoted by the media. I felt a spokesperson for me and others like myself, who were the despised believers of the world, had emerged.

The argument against Billy Graham was that he was flirting with modernism and compromising the gospel through his "cooperative evangelism." As an eighteen-year-old college student, I didn't have the wisdom nor the experience to deal with these assertions. But deep down within myself I could not believe what I was hearing. Yet, in the years to come I was to hear many others say the same thing. I was always troubled by second-degree separationism, which taught that "true"

Christians must not only separate from the liberals of the mainline church, but also from those evangelicals like Billy Graham who were compromising the true church by their association with these apostate ministers.

Why, I wondered, were we always so busy defining the perimeters in which truth and a right relationship to God were accurately defined? Was it really possible, I wondered, to have a pure church? The more I thought about this, the more I felt that to be truly pure was an impossibility. The sheer logic of it creates split after split and an arrogance on the part of the splinter toward those who choose to remain. How can anyone except God himself be pure and uncontaminated from false belief, ethical error, and incomplete judgment? For me the so-called concept of the purity of the church was a straitjacket that made me increasingly uncomfortable. It stifled my experience of the whole church and made me an outsider to the church through the ages.

The Ecumenical Movement

I was a graduate student at Concordia Theological Seminary between 1965 and 1968. And it was here that I took my first course in the ecumenical movement. I still remember the tension I experienced as I faced some of the issues about the unity of the Church of Jesus Christ.

Jesus' prayer in John 17, when he prayed "they may be one," impressed me and I have often referred to that prayer. Once, an evangelical who is strongly opposed to the concern for the unity of the church responded to my quotation of John 17 with the words, "But that is only mentioned once in scripture." I reminded him that the phrase "Ye must be born again" is also mentioned only once, but we have built a whole Christian tradition around it.

I was also impressed with the emphasis given to the unity of the church by the early church fathers. Clement of Rome, writing to the Christians of Corinth about a split in their church, said, "Why do we divide and tear to pieces the members of Christ, and raise up such strife against our own body . . . as to forget that we are members of one another?" Ignatius, Cyprian, Augustine, and others who wrote about the church expressed a similar concern. Cyprian, for example, saw the church as the "seamless robe" of Christ and illustrated how we could see the unity of the church as coming from its source. He reminded his readers that though there were many rivers there was only one source of water, and though there were many rays of the sun there was only one source of light. Another favorite image of the church is captured by Irenaeus, a second-century writer, in his statement, "The church . . . although scattered throughout the whole world . . . believes just as if she had one soul and one and the same heart." These words compelled me to examine my separatist attitude and to think about the church in a more global sense. I began to see more clearly the tragedy of the Reformation and longed for a reversal of those attitudes that separated me from my brothers and sisters in other denominations and expressions of the faith.

As I studied modern history, I saw how natural it was after the Reformation to harden the lines between groups of Christian people. I noticed, for example, that churches became set in their patterns, and that a unity between certain denominations and a national identity was established.

It seemed to me that Catholics were Italian and Polish, that Lutherans were German and Scandinavian, that the English were Anglican, and that the Scots were Presbyterian. Free churches and new denominations emerged in all of these countries as they broke away from the state church under the conviction of separation of the church from secular control.

Gradually the various groups broke communication with one another and sought independence. They came to America to set up their distinct denominations, with their individual institutions and agencies, with very little cooperation or spirit of unity among them.

I was particularly interested to discover that the initial impulse toward ecumenicalism occurred on the mission field among evangelical Christians. Here, people from Anglican, Baptist, Lutheran, Methodist, and other traditions were working in competition with one another for the conversion of the same people. The absurdity of the situation was met with an attempt to unify the activities of the missionaries. This effort gradually grew into the present-day ecumenical movement.

It is true that the liberal element in the Protestant church took over the ecumenical movement in the middle of this century. As evangelicals broke away from mainline denominations starting in the 1920s, they carried with them a perception that the ecumenical movement was something that was not only liberal but also dangerous and to be avoided.

In recent years many evangelicals have acknowledged that a significant shift away from a liberal theology toward apostolic Christianity has been occurring within the halls of the World Council of Churches and the National Council of Churches.

Evangelicals like Dr. Richard Lovelace, (emeritus) profes-sor of church history at Gordon-Conwell Theological Semi-nary in Massachusetts and leader in the Council on Christian Union, are giving evangelicals a new voice in ecumenical cir-cles. In a recent interview with Dr. Lovelace, he said, "When I was a seminarian at Westminster, I kept asking myself, 'What's the right denomination?' and the only answer I could get out of scripture was that there is no right denomination. They're all wrong. The whole system is wrong."

My own model of an ecumenical spirit in the twenti-eth century is Billy Graham. Dr. Graham exhibits a spirit of love toward Christians of all sorts. He has worked with every Protestant denomination; he has made friends in the Ortho-dox church as well as in the Catholic church. He has moved with great spiritual agility within all these traditions.

I think we must ask why Dr. Graham has been able to demonstrate an ecumenical spirit and embrace these tradi-tions and have members of the various traditions embrace him in return.

I believe it comes down to the fact that Dr. Graham is con-cerned about preaching the gospel of Jesus Christ without getting caught up in the trappings of culture and national identity that each denomination carries. He is able to accent the transcultural aspect of the gospel that one finds in every believing tradition. The simple fact is that when we peel away the secondary layers of tradition, we are able to get back to the apostolic interpretation given to the Christ-event.

My problem with those who fight against the unity of the church is that they often do so on the grounds of second-ary issues. We may not all agree that the Bible is inerrant, but we can agree that it is the authoritative apostolic witness to Jesus Christ. We may not be able to agree on our specific interpretation of bread and wine, but we can at least agree that they are the symbols of Christ living, dying, and rising again for our salvation. We may not be able to agree on our specific interpretation and practice of baptism, but we ought to be able to agree that this is God's sign to us of his grace and love toward us. We may not be able to agree on the specifics of the end times, but we can agree on the coming again of Christ.

■ ■ ■

In the Episcopal Church I find a healthy sense of unity and diversity. In this tradition we recognize that that which holds the church together is more important than that which divides the church.

I like to view the church as a house that is built upon certain pillars. Its pillars include the scripture, the early creeds, the sacraments, the order of oversight, ministry and service, worship, and a responsibility for the life of the world. Although there may be diversity within these areas, we are united in matters of faith.

My choice is to stress this unity and acknowledge our differences as the human and cultural element of the church. I want to both affirm all God's people everywhere and seek to understand, affirm, and enjoy the differences between us. I can do this in the Episcopal Church.

CHAPTER

6

Growing into
a Holistic Spirituality

I grew up Pentecostal, so powerful spiritual experiences were par for the course. But when I received Eucharist from a priest for the first time, and he said, "Body of Christ," I was shocked to tears. God's presence, in a hunk of bread I was chewing? The candles, the musty carpet, the priest's lisp—it was all so earthy. And I was terribly hungry for that.

—*Amber Noel (M. Div.), Member, All Saints Anglican Church, Durham, North Carolina*

In the fall of 1983, Bishop Jon Braun of the Evangelical Orthodox church wrote and told me he was coming through Wheaton. "Could we get together?" he asked. I not only wanted to get together with him, I wanted him to talk to my class about his pilgrimage into Orthodoxy because we were studying the Orthodox church at that time.

In the course of his lecture he made a comment that has stuck with me. I want to share it with you. He was speaking about his upbringing in a Christian home and the fact that as a young person he had always believed but had had no dramatic experience of salvation. His parents, anxious for him to have a dramatic conversion experience, began to push him toward a decision. "This," he said soberly, "actually pushed me out of the church and made me think for a temporary period of time that I was an unbeliever." He then went on to say that placing too much emphasis on a dateable experience of salvation can be dangerous if we do not take into account that many who grow up in Christian homes grow into faith without such an experience. When they are forced toward a decision they have already made quietly, they may begin to think of themselves as unbelievers.

This illustration points to the tension between the spirituality of justification and sanctification. Both aspects of believing in Christ and growing in Christ are complementary to each other.

A Spirituality of Conversion

Evangelicals are strong in the spirituality of conversion. Evangelical history is in itself a history of those spurts of revival that have dotted the church through the ages. We stand in the tradition of Justin Martyr, Gregory of Nyssa, St. Francis of Assisi, John Wycliffe, Martin Luther, John Wesley, Jonathan Edwards, D.L. Moody, and many others who have experienced a dramatic encounter with Jesus Christ.

Certainly, a dramatic experience of the saving reality of Christ is not to be denied or minimized. Such an experience born of God by the power of the Holy Spirit makes a powerful impact on the personality and has the positive effect of making one see life through new eyes. It is not unusual to find people leaving the liturgical tradition because of its failure to stress conversion adequately. On the other hand, it is not unusual to find evangelicals leaving evangelical churches because they overstress conversion and inadequately emphasize growth in

Christ. Let me describe some of those approaches to spirituality within evangelicalism that some of us find inadequate.

A Spirituality of Dos and Don'ts

My first memory of a post-conversion spirituality is what I call a spirituality of dos and don'ts. As far back as I can remember, the dos were: read your bible every day, pray daily, witness to other people, stay away from evil haunts, keep yourself pure, and get involved in the local church. The don'ts were just as clear: don't smoke, dance, drink, go to the theater, or play cards.

I am not totally against a spirituality of dos and don'ts. New Testament writers give evidence of a similar kind of spirituality among the early Christians. In Galatians 5, Paul states, "Do not walk after the flesh." Then he gives a list of those sins of the flesh that Christians should avoid. In the same passage he admonishes the Christian convert to "walk after the Spirit," after which he lists the fruits of the Spirit. Paul gives a similar negative and positive list in Colossians 3, where he admonishes new Christians to "put off the old man" and to "put on the new man." This same concept of a contrasting list of dos and don'ts is found in early Christian literature, such as the *Didache* written around 100 A.D. Scholars recognize these lists as instructions surrounding baptism. It has been strongly suggested that memorizing lists that guide behavior and attempting to live by the rules implied within them may have a positive effect on Christian life.

What I and others like me find objectionable are the man-made rules that have grown out of the New Testament spirituality. When rules against smoking, drinking, and dancing are turned into absolutes, they cheapen true spirituality. They make spirituality too simple because they bypass the weightier matters such as concern for justice. The list is what Dietrich Bonhoeffer, the important German theologian, called a cheap grace. It is a set of rules that is fairly easy to follow.

In my experience I have found that people often live by these rules because they feel pressured from the group that demands conformity, rather than committed from the heart. Let me give you an example. At Bob Jones University I was a "preacher boy." A preacher boy was any student who was planning to go into some form of ministry. All future Christian workers (male only) met once a week in the preacher boys' class and were given practical instruction on how to build a church, run a Sunday school, and things of that sort. In addition to our weekly meeting, we were required to witness to seven people a week and hand in a report detailing our conversation and the results.

There were close to one thousand students in that class. If you multiply that by seven, it means that seven thousand witnesses a week for thirty-four weeks of the year were being made by preacher boys alone. That's two hundred and thirty-eight thousand contacts a year in the environs of Greenville, South Carolina!

Now, there were times that I was committed and I fulfilled the spirit of that expectation. I often went away for weekends to work in a local church and community. Frequently these jaunts proved very positive. However, there were other times, which were more frequent than I care to admit, when I had a paper or an exam pressing me. These times were characterized by a quick trip to Greenville with seven tracts. I would simply hand out the tract and say, "Are you saved?" hoping the person would not want to engage in a long conversation. I'd then hastily write up my report and turn it in to satisfy the requirement of being a witness.

To say that my conscience bothered me about this approach to witnessing is an understatement. I'm still sensitive about this kind of impersonal witness and uncomfortable with personal witnessing in general. Keeping the rule in this instance undermined the sheer joy of being a witness because I was acting under pressure rather than from the heart. Similar responses can be seen anytime the letter of the law is pressed too far.

A Spirituality of Believing the Right Thing

In seminary and graduate school, I encountered another kind of spirituality that I will call an intellectual spirituality of believing the right doctrine. Again, like the spirituality of dos and don'ts, there is a biblical basis to the spirituality of correct doctrine. This kind of spirituality is found in the writings of Paul, especially when he admonishes the early Christians not to follow after the heresies that were already arising in the first century. In the Pastoral Epistles, in Colossians, and in other passages, he urges Christians to stand fast in the truth that has been handed down from the apostles.

For example, in 1 Corinthians 15:3–4, Paul is battling with a faction in the church that is denying the bodily resurrection of Jesus from the dead. He appeals to these people to hold fast to the tradition of truth he handed over to them.

Then he reminds his readers about the message he delivered to them: "For I delivered to you as of first importance what I also received, that Christ died for our sins in accordance with the scriptures, that he was buried, that he was raised on the third day in accordance with the scriptures."

I think it is generally agreed that the content of the Apostles' Creed represents an essential summary of apostolic Christianity. Early Christians learned this creed in preparation for baptism; and when they were baptized, they were not only baptized in the name of the Father, Son, and Holy Spirit, but also in the simple truths about the Triune God proclaimed in the Apostles' Creed. (An early form of this creed, structured in a question and answer format for use with candidates for baptism, can be found in the document known as *The Apostolic Tradition* from the third century.)

But the kind of spirituality of right doctrine to which I refer goes beyond the basic affirmation of faith and into a particular and precise interpretation of the faith. Let me give you an example of what I mean. Recently I was a guest speaker at a church in the Midwest. The people in this particular congregation very consciously adhere to strict Calvinism, especially on the issue of the sovereignty of God, the question of election, and God's providence. Before I spoke, I had dinner with several of the church's elders. During our conversation, I was asked a number of leading questions, which I could tell were tests of my spiritual orthodoxy. Although the people were most kind and gracious, these questions made me uncomfortable. I didn't feel that I was being accepted for my faith in Christ. Rather, I felt as if I was being examined for my adherence to a particular system of interpreting Christ. I thought my answers were not totally acceptable. And I began to feel like an outsider rather than a welcomed member of the group.

One tragic aspect of the spirituality of right doctrine is that it tends to create a uniformity of interpretation that stifles growth. Recently, I was talking to a student who transferred to Wheaton College from a fundamentalist college. I asked him, "Tony, how does Wheaton differ from your other educational experience?"

"Well, to tell you the truth, it's a breath of fresh air," he said.

"How so?" I responded with curiosity.

"I'm allowed to think here."

"What do you mean?" I asked, my curiosity growing by the second.

"In my Bible classes at the other college, I began to question some of the interpretations of the institution. I simply wanted answers to some very honest questions about why we believe and practice certain things. The answers I was getting were not satisfactory. So I pushed harder."

"You challenged the professor?"

"Right. I don't think I was obnoxious about it. But apparently the teacher felt the questions were evidence that I was falling away from the truth."

"Why, what happened?"

"He called me into his office for a special session."

"Yes."

"He said, 'Tony, I'm really worried about you. You seem to be slipping spiritually. I'd like to have prayer with you and ask God to get hold of your life again.'"

"And how did you interpret that?"

"It was obvious to me and clear from our conversation that questioning was unacceptable. What is truly spiritual is believing what you are told. A questioning spirit is a doubting spirit and a doubting spirit comes from an unbelieving heart. That's what it boils down to."

Unfortunately, this kind of conversation could be repeated thousands of times. The mentality of the spirituality of right belief can become, as it did for Tony, a stifling experience of not being able to show some healthy doubt about the faith or its particular denominational interpretation. It is not uncommon for doubters to learn how to keep their mouth shut to keep out of trouble. The tragedy of this approach to spirituality is that it leads to a mouthing of the faith that lacks integrity.

In the Anglican tradition I have found a freedom of curiosity and openness. I regularly speak in Episcopal churches where, during the discussion, a considerable number of viewpoints will be expressed openly and forcefully. I've found a give and take on the local parish level that is healthy and dynamic.

An Ethical Spirituality

In the late '60s and early '70s, I first encountered what I will call an ethical spirituality. I speak particularly of the spirituality that is concerned for the poor, the oppressed, and the downtrodden.

Certainly ethical spirituality is a strong and even central motif in the life and teachings of Jesus. His mission was chiefly to the poor, to the outcasts of society.

In the late '60s, the civil rights movement and opposition to the war in Vietnam, together with an exposure to economic injustice in this country and political imperialism around the world, caused many an evangelical's consciousness to be raised.

Jim Wallis, the editor of *Sojourners*, was a student at that time at Trinity Seminary in Deerfield, Illinois. John Alexander, the editor of *The Other Side*, was teaching philosophy at Wheaton College. Both of these young men were friends of mine, and they began to expand my conscience and sense of Christian ethical responsibility.

In the fall of 1973, Jim Wallis and John Alexander, together with Ron Sider and others, organized a number of evangelicals to meet at the old YMCA building in Chicago to discuss the evangelical conscience in the face of growing national and worldwide issues of ethical importance. Out of that conference came the historic Chicago Declaration, a forthright call to evangelicals to embrace an ethical spirituality.

All of us at the conference were organized into various groups for discussion. I was assigned to the economic responsibility group. I remember how appalled I was at the discussion. The issue at stake was the meaning of Jesus' words, "Take up your cross and follow after me." The specific question under debate was. "Could one be rich and be a Christian?" The word "rich" was never really defined then, so it is difficult for me now to state categorically what was meant by the term. But one of the members of the group was a man very interested in social issues. He also happened to be a successful businessman. He shared with us that his salary was over $100,000 a year (in 2012 worth about $210,000), that he drove a Mercedes-Benz, and that he owned a small yacht. Could he qualify as a Christian? His question was sincere. Finally we went around the circle and each person responded to the gentleman's question. The consensus was that if he really wanted to follow after Jesus, he would need to give up his job, sell his belongings, and give the proceeds to the poor. Then he would be in a position to follow after Christ.

I firmly believe in ethical spirituality, but in this case I felt it was carried too far. Like the other kinds of spirituality I had encountered in my pilgrimage, ethical spirituality was being turned into something legalistic and wooden. It was coming from the outside asking for a legal conformity to a set of man-made rules.

I do not judge Jim Wallis, John Alexander, or Ron Sider. Although they have taken personal vows to live on a poverty level, I don't feel that they negatively judge others who have not chosen to follow an ethical spirituality to this degree. What I am concerned about is the legalistic interpretation that others have made from this lifestyle choice.

A Spirituality of Experience

More recently I have come into contact with what I will call the spirituality of experience in the Anglican tradition. I and others like myself are increasingly attracted to this particular form of spirituality. It is not a substitute for the other spiritualities I have described. Rather, it is complementary to them and contains them all in its larger orbit.

I can best define the spirituality of experience by describing it as the attempt to integrate Christ with all of life. Let me describe three forms of this spiritual experience that have attracted me toward the Episcopal spiritual tradition.

It was in the context of the Episcopal Church that I first heard of the Jesus prayer. Although the Jesus prayer is primarily an Eastern Orthodox form of spirituality, it has also been accepted in the West by Catholics and Anglicans. The Jesus prayer is the simple prayer, "Lord Jesus Christ, Son of God, have mercy on me a sinner."

The prayer originates from the attitude of the penitent sinner who prayed, "Lord, have mercy on me a sinner," a prayer that becomes clearer when contrasted to the prayer of the Pharisee who said, "Lord, I thank thee that I am not as these others, publicans and sinners."

It is a prayer of the heart, an attitude prayer that gained prominence as a lay devotion in the Eastern church. It has some similarities to Brother Andrew's "practicing the presence of God."

The prayer is to be repeated again and again as a means of establishing a continuing relationship with God. It is short enough to be said with the beat of the heart. To this day, people who use this form of prayer will sometimes rest their chin on their chest and allow their eyes to gaze on the area of the heart as a symbol of uniting both head and heart and thus the whole person in the prayer.

The content of the prayer is thoroughly evangelical. It affirms the full title of Christ, acknowledges our sin, and assures us of his mercy. I often find myself saying this prayer as I walk or drive or as I lie down to sleep. I feel the presence of Christ through this prayer—a unity with him and his saving action for me.

Another thoroughly Christ-centered spirituality that attracts me to the Anglican tradition is what has been called

Eucharistic spirituality. This is a spirituality born of the conviction that the Eucharist represents the saving action of Christ at work. I have already referred to a supernatural understanding of the Eucharist in the Anglican tradition, a prerequisite, I believe, for the experience of Eucharistic spirituality.

Eucharistic spirituality is the experience of being spiritually nourished and strengthened by eating the bread and drinking the wine. Since I perceive this as God doing something for me, I find myself drawn to the Eucharist as a necessary part of my spiritual diet. The mystery of what Christ did for me on the cross reaches into my inner person in a way that I cannot describe.

John Calvin described the Eucharist as a "sign," a "pledge," a "testimony" of God's work on our behalf. These are nouns that imply an action. I can now understand these terms of Calvin, not because I have intellectualized them, but because I have experienced internally the power of Christ's action for me.

In the Eucharist I feel both saved again and compelled to live in the Eucharistic way. Both justification and sanctification are communicated to me. Bread and wine speaks to me of my sin. But it at once communicates the saving reality of Christ. I am caught up in its power and cleansed by the fresh work of the Holy Spirit which I continually experience at that Table of Communion.

A third spirituality of experience is the discipline of following the church year as a personal devotion. I've always had a difficult time maintaining a continuous devotion in my life. Like others, I've probably tried everything in the book.

The church year is a schedule for living through the life of Christ in a systematic way. It begins with Advent, when scripture readings and the corporate life of the church begin to center on the coming birth of Christ. During this time, my life is directed toward a more spiritual experience of Christmas because I am called upon both individually and within the corporate worshiping community to center on the coming of Christ. During Christmas, which lasts for twelve days, not just one, I am led into a fuller experience of the babe born in Bethlehem. And during Epiphany, the season that celebrates the manifestation of Christ to the world, I am personally and corporately drawn into the witness of Christ and his church to the world.

The period from Advent to Epiphany drops off in intensity after January 6 until the beginning of Lent on Ash Wednesday. Lent begins a very intense period of personal spiritual examination, which leads toward renewal and deeper faith. Lent is a time to reflect deeply on my personal relationship to Christ. It is a different spiritual experience than that of Advent, Christmas, or Epiphany. During Lent I am called upon to enter into the sufferings of Jesus and to prepare for his death.

For me, this discipline has made Holy Week and Easter an experience of spiritual vigor and joy that goes far beyond my old attitude of "Oops, here it is Easter, already." Preparation for Easter that takes me into the tomb has given me a much more vital spiritual participation in the resurrection of Christ, and a deeper sense and experience of that resurrection joy, which I celebrate individually and corporately until Pentecost. During Pentecost season, the emphasis shifts to the power of the Holy Spirit that brings the church into existence. I am called upon to receive the Holy Spirit's power anew and to engage myself in the study of the Epistles.

What I like most is the variety in spiritual experience that is given to me in the discipline following the church year. Further, the fact that the whole church is celebrating the same events provides a leadership in spirituality that is outside of my own meager efforts. I join with other pilgrims in the faith as together we reenact the significant moments in the life of Christ that draw us into unity with him and with his purpose.

■ ■ ■

I find when most people are honest about their spiritual pilgrimage, they admit to the difficulty of maintaining the habit of a spiritual discipline. What attracts me most about the Anglican spiritual tradition is that it provides purposeful spiritual direction in the life of Christ. And I am not alone. Others are walking the same path with me, assisting me on my way, helping me when I fail, encouraging me in the journey we are taking together. Therefore, other pilgrims on the Canterbury Trail will share their stories in the next section of the book.

PART

2

Other Pilgrims Share Their Stories

CHAPTER

7

Anna Masi

The first time I experienced Anglican liturgy, I felt relieved. Just shy of my twentieth birthday, I wandered into an Anglican church down the street from my university as a last-ditch effort to salvage the remains of what little faith I had left. Growing up I heard all the statistics from my youth pastor: "Seventy-six percent of all young people lose their faith in college," he would say over and over again, "Do you want to be a statistic?" I have absolutely no idea if those numbers are accurate or from where he even got them, but I do remember sitting in youth group, hearing it and thinking, "No, that won't be me."

At the age of 18, I had left for college (Florida State University in Tallahassee) determined to make it to the other side of baccalaureate stainless and strong. So when I found myself in May of my sophomore year standing and sitting and kneeling—and sitting and standing again—with several hundred complete strangers, not only had I long since feared that God had disappeared, I had never been so exhausted.

■ ■ ■

I grew up in a small, sleepy resort town in South Florida. A paradise getaway for the wealthy, my hometown remained mostly off the radar from any major excitement or out-of-the-ordinary activity. When I was growing up, the major talk of the town revolved around the erection of our very own mega-church. Though my family is Methodist, at the age of 12, I became one of the hundreds of kids who attended youth group there, and until I graduated high school it was my only source of exposure to Christianity.

Complete with a skateboard park in the back, the youth had their own building, which contained two massive worship rooms—one for middle school and one for high school—that were separated by a game room and snack bar. Each worship room had black walls, state-of-the-art light and sound systems, and a stage for their worship bands.

Youth group was exciting, and I attended as many trips and retreats as I could. It was on one such trip, when I was 14, that my involvement with this youth group changed dramatically from social outlet to spiritual commitment. We were on our way to Denver, and somewhere on the long stretches of empty highway out West, while reading the Bible and journaling, the world grew immeasurably vast in an instant. The story of God seemed so big, so endless, and I was so small in it. And yet, I was in it. I had a place.

From then on I was hooked. At youth group and on retreats we had "mountain-top experiences"—emotional storms during worship—in which we danced, fell to our knees, raised our hands, and cried. These vulnerable moments before God and one another prompted us to re-dedicate our lives to Christ and fueled us during the week at school as we interacted with peers.

Over time I underwent a great deal of formation. I learned the spiritual dangers of engaging in any improper behavior. The leaders emphasized purity in all aspects of life, as lack of pure behavior signaled inner rebellion against God as well as threatened our witness to the outside world.

As time wore on, I began struggling to maintain many of the ideal standards of what made a girl into a "godly woman." The struggle was more inward than behavioral, as I refrained from partying with friends and vowed to wait until marriage, but often felt confronted with the reality of my heart's inability to attain ideal desires willfully or joyfully. All of our desire should be for God alone; desire for anything else was wrongly ordered.

This stumped me repeatedly. For example, because we were teenagers the most popular sermon topic was sexual purity. Romantic desire of any kind was only proper in marriage, so those waiting until marriage were urged to suppress that part of one's self, physically and emotionally, until then. While in many ways this felt right, I worried that I might never marry. Then what? Would I be left in a "holding pattern," waiting indefinitely?

In spite of this, however, I desperately longed to please and desire God above all else. I believed purity of heart to be a true good, so I worked to seek after the Lord in all things, hoping that God would satisfy any and all unmet wants in due time. I also felt called to ministry, and intended to follow it no matter the cost.

■ ■ ■

When I arrived for college at Florida State University, I fell in immediately with a campus ministry similar to my home church. In this group I worked ever harder to "submit," to "surrender," to be transformed into a true godly woman. But as my freshman year came to a close, my frustration and simultaneous guilt at my own inability to attain the ideal peaked. I spent so much energy pushing things down from within, at some point I realized that I could no longer weed-out what about my person was good and admissible, and what was bad and in need of correction. I felt suffocated.

At the end of my freshman year I had also decided to switch my major to Religion after taking an introductory Old Testament course. When I returned from the summer to my sophomore year, many of my friends in the campus ministry expressed mixed views about my major. They urged me to be on my guard. They warned that studying religion in a state university could cause me to "lose my faith." However, I dismissed their warnings, and began pulling away, decreasing my involvement in the community.

Over the course of that first semester, my faith *did* begin to crumble. I refused to tell anyone what was happening, partly from stubbornness, and partly because I knew immediately *why* it was crumbling—and it had nothing to do with professors. Nor, in fact, was it difficult theological questions I was suddenly faced with, or scribal errors in the biblical texts, or even the complex messes of anti-Semitism, the oppression of women, or the holy wars. Rather, I began to lose my faith because I realized I was studying Christianity, but everything I learned looked nothing like the religion I had always known.

Martyrs, creeds, saints, desert fathers, theological councils, liturgy, eschatology, women mystics, ancient rituals, sacraments—I suddenly found myself confronted by entire empires of people about whom I had never known. I did not recognize my own religion, and I panicked. Once I saw the differences between what I studied and my experiences, I immediately spiraled into confusion over whether or not "Christian" was a title I wanted. I felt as though the curtain had been pulled back, revealing what everyone else had always known about Christianity; the joke was on me.

The confusion soon became so overwhelming that I grew increasingly afraid—and then incredibly angry. Soon I severed ties entirely with anyone associated with my evangelical life, from my home church to the campus ministry. Those I did not suspect of malice I reduced to ignorance, leaving them to their fate of being led blindly for the rest of their days. By the time I started spring semester of my sophomore year, I was without community, without a church, or virtually anyone associated with my religion whom I trusted.

The greatest difficulty I experienced was the literal crumbling of my relationship with God: I did not stop believing in God; rather, I feared God had left. And when God disappeared, everything else—my hopes for the future, my call to ministry, my day-to-day life—all of that disappeared, too. And that's when I began to suffer anxiety attacks, because it was just me, sitting at the edge of the bed, and I couldn't feel God with me.

Then I met Matt. We had two classes together spring semester sophomore year and walked to class together each day. Matt was Catholic, and though in youth group growing up I had been told that Catholics were not real Christians, everything about him broke down my prejudices.

I did not tell him what was happening; he was the only stable connection to Christianity I had, and I feared telling him would drive a wedge between us. The time spent walking to class became precious conversation time for us. We talked mostly about class and friends, but often we talked about faith. Well, really he talked about faith and I listened. I hung onto what he said like it was water in the desert.

Matt never preached—he just thought out loud. But when he spoke I heard martyrs; I heard tradition; I heard fearless struggling; I heard assurance; I heard another world. It was as though he'd been abstracted from elsewhere, from some far-off place I'd always longed for but had never been, and he'd brought a bit of that place with him.

By spring break my anxiety attacks stopped. Around that same time, Matt, who was an English major and graduating that semester, finally answered the one question he had always avoided every time I asked.

"So what *do* you want to be when you grow up?" I teased him.

And finally one day he said, "A monk."

"Oh," I looked at him a little shocked, and then I smiled. "Okay then."

Once he made his big confession, our friendship grew stronger. He began to speak openly about his desire for the monastic life and all it entailed, and I begged to hear about it. Though springtime is the rainy season in Tallahassee, whenever I think about that semester, every memory I recall is sunny.

After he graduated, we wrote e-mails weekly to keep in touch. And by mid-summer, though I still felt general suspicion and anger toward most churches and Christians—pastors especially—I decided to give church another try. I considered the Catholic churches in town, but ultimately could not bring myself to attend. Matt had broken down most of my prejudices, but not all of them, and I was still unsure. I had, however, befriended several Episcopalians my freshman year, and for a brief period attended their campus ministry services. My little experience of the denomination felt Catholic enough to satisfy my cravings, but Protestant enough to feel comfortable. Since by this time most of those friends no longer attended there, and I hesitated to get involved in *any* campus ministry again, I picked a random Anglican church a few miles from campus, walked in on a Tuesday afternoon to the church office, and asked to speak to a priest.

St. Peter's Anglican Church sits on a main highway near downtown. All brick and rather unassuming, the building is in the typical southern-style church architecture, with seasonal flowers planted around the church and a sign displaying only their weekly service times in small print. At my request the receptionist sent over the college priest, Father John. In his mid-thirties at the time, Father John stood at least two heads taller than me, with brown hair, a round face, and glasses. He greeted me with a smile, asked how he could help, and I asked if we could speak somewhere privately. We settled into a side office, gave introductions, and immediately launched into the reason I was there.

"So what can I do for you?" he inquired politely.

"I'm just wondering what you all believe before I waste my time coming to your services," I spat back. Father John raised his eyebrows slightly, but remained composed.

"Well, that's a broad question," he replied, "perhaps you can—"

"Look, you can skip the part about Jesus dying for my sins," I interrupted, waving my hands over-dramatically as I spoke, "because I get it." Father John shuffled in his seat, gave me a searching look, and then suddenly leaned back in his chair and began.

He told me that St. Peter's was a church that was not here for my entertainment, but welcomes me if I ever want to join them for worship. He told me they believed in the Trinity, welcomed any and all questions, and were a church that took their sacramental life very seriously. He told me that what they believed as Anglicans and the importance of understanding their identity as a community. And then, after several more minutes, he told me the times of the Sunday services.

"You're welcome to join us any time," he repeated, never breaking his polite expression. "Did you have any other questions?"

"No," I huffed. I didn't particularly like him, but I liked his answer, not because I knew whether or not I agreed with his beliefs, but because he did not seem bothered if I disagreed. He wasn't rude, but he was sure, which both intrigued and annoyed me. I thanked him for his time and left, but when I saw him the next day at a local coffee shop, I blatantly ignored him.

I attended St. Peter's alone that Sunday. I hesitantly took a seat about midway up the pews. Because of my brief experience at the Episcopal campus ministry, I had some idea of what to expect, but on the whole what proceeded was foreign. We stood, sat, knelt, sat, stood, sat, and stood again. I knew no one on my right or left. As the service began, I wondered whether I should be feeling anything—some kind of emotion or welling up to let me know God was there or that this was really worship. I felt nothing.

Then about halfway through the service, we pulled down the kneelers and knelt for the Prayers of the People. I did not read along with everyone, but instead just placed my elbows on the pew in front of me, folded my hands together, rested my forehead on my hands, and closed my eyes.

"For all people in their daily life and work," a priest's voice carried over the room.

And the voices around me replied, "For our families, friends, and neighbors, and for those who are alone."

And for those who are alone. The words echoed in my head. I immediately opened my eyes and glanced at the people on either side of me, still locked in prayer. Some were reading from the book in front of them; others had their eyes closed, praying from memory. *They just prayed for me,* I thought. *Everyone in this room just prayed for me, and they have no idea.* And suddenly, I did not feel great emotion or an intense welling-up, but overwhelming relief. None of this service relied on me in order to be efficacious, to be legitimate. And when I did not have it within me to participate, those around me spoke on my behalf. My muscles relaxed, my arms slipped down from the pew, dropping my hands onto my lap, and I sunk even deeper onto the kneeler.

"Hear us, Lord," the priest called.

"For your mercy is great," they replied.

I attended St. Peter's every Sunday for six months without associating with much of anyone, ordained or lay. I slowly gained acquaintance with individuals who sat near my regular pew, and said hello or made light conversation after the service with faces that slowly grew more familiar, but I still refused to become involved in any Bible studies or groups.

■ ■ ■

Unfortunately, while I slowly felt like I had found what I'd been looking for, my suspicion of "church people" and all clergy still held. A part of me felt like any minute the bottom was going to fall out, that this wasn't really what I hoped it was. At any moment I was going to find out they were hiding something, they were lying, or that in spite of the "smells and bells," they really were just like everyone else.

The liturgy, however, was another story. I was addicted. I began to crave the smell of incense during the week, and I began mimicking the up-and-down prayer routine in my own prayer times at home. My body began to take on a rhythm, a beat I could set my internal clock by to live my day-to-day life. And it wasn't just that my body began to follow this rhythm; it was that I noticed my body at all.

And I did. *Constantly.* Each week I discovered a new body part I did not know I had. I will never forget the Sunday it started: it was my hands during communion. It was simple, really. Right over left, or left over right? Or did it matter? I focused on this intently for weeks. I watched others go up for communion and how they placed their hands. Then it was my knees on the kneeler: should it be just the tip of the knees while I keep my legs straight? Can I sit on the edge of my pew and simply rest my knees on the kneeler? Then I discovered touch points on my head, shoulders, and chest;

every time we crossed ourselves, the thump of my fingers on my body lingered for moments afterward. *Again,* I thought. *Let's do it again.*

It wasn't that I felt a legalistic need to get all of the movement just right or to be perfect in the service. Rather, limb-by-limb, I excitedly discovered that my whole body, not just my mind or my emotions, could participate in worship. My body gained dignity in the liturgy, a wholeness and a value I had never experienced before. Suddenly I had the language to articulate my beliefs because the language was no longer limited.

For instance, consider the difference between "waiting until marriage" and "being celibate." Those who are waiting until marriage are all celibate, but not all who are celibate are waiting until marriage. I am celibate, not because I feel commanded by God to "stay pure" for my future spouse or to suppress some kind of wrongly ordered sexual desire of my body. I am celibate because my body is the physical manifestation of the reality ushered in through the crucifixion and resurrection; and I am whole, redeemed, and complete just as I am through Christ alone. I am not waiting for anything.

Likewise, as I gained my own body, I slowly realized that I also gained the bodies of those around me. The hands I opened to receive communion I first opened to receive other hands in the passing of the Peace. I swallowed the bread and wine, and then carried it out with me into the city, to friends' houses for lunch, and into my home. Priests were no longer points of suspicion, but walking sacraments, bodies ordained and set apart. The liturgy, in other words, had arms and legs, and those arms and legs were ours.

Finally, as we approached Christmas time that year, I began to let go and get involved in the St. Peter's community. By the following summer I found myself with Father John and five others in the middle of East Africa. When I returned, I began an internship under another priest with the youth ministry. By the following May, I had reaffirmed my baptismal vows in front of the entire congregation, been confirmed, and then commissioned as a seminarian on behalf of our church and the diocese. I left for Duke Divinity School that July.

On my last Sunday at St. Peter's, Father John gave the announcements at service. I was sitting in my usual pew.

"Just over two years ago, a young girl came into the office at St. Peter's and asked to speak to a priest," he began. I closed my eyes and held my breath. "And now she is leaving us and going on to seminary," he continued, "and we could not be more proud." I exhaled, looked up at him, and smiled. That day during the Prayers of the People, I actually did know who was sitting on either side of me, and I prayed fervently for my family, friends, and neighbors. But more so I prayed for those who are alone, just in case.

8

Stefany Webber Welch

66 "When you're feeling out-of-sorts, flee—FLEE, I say—to the Eucharist!"

So goes a classic Bob Webber quote, one I heard him say many times. He said it in class as my professor, usually with a dramatic flair—his resemblance to Albert Einstein in full flower—hair wildly flying in all directions, eyes wide and serious, and hands curled into fists, pounding the air. (He always knew how to be serious and funny at the same time.) He also said it to me in private, as my dad, in a gentler, more fatherly fashion, encouraging me to seek the supernatural help that no one else could give.

When I was five years old, the Webber family, including me, joined St. Barnabas Episcopal Church in Glen Ellyn, Illinois. I recall the hard wooden pews, the dimly lit half-circle sanctuary, and the musty-sweet smell of incense hanging in the air. I recall listening intently to the beautiful organ music, as I observed people singing the liturgy, standing, sitting, kneeling, praying, my curious little eyes taking it all in, all of my senses heightened. I remember taking the bread and sipping the Eucharistic wine. Everything was cloaked in mystery and meaning. It felt like a little cocoon, a safe place.

This set the stage for my definition of "church." Growing up, church was something our family did every Sunday, rain or shine. The routine of a church-going life was woven into the fabric of my being. Church, faith, and the search for meaning and mystery was a thread I would follow into my adult life. We made a couple of church re-locations over the years and eventually found a spiritual home at St. Mark's Episcopal Church in Geneva, Illinois, when I was in junior high school. I loved the comfort and the routine of the liturgy. I valued the reverence and the awe. It felt like God was just distant enough from me that he belonged to everyone.

In contrast to that, it became clear to me as I grew in understanding my faith, that many of my Christian friends related more to God's immanence. I admit there were times when I found this superficial. I felt that their perception lacked depth, as if their personal relationship to Jesus was the ultimate goal and that Jesus had died only for them.

I sometimes wondered if spirituality was a popularity contest, and I was losing because I didn't express my faith with the same words, or even the same assurance. I was a bit timid about my relationship with God, with an attitude of "I really love God, and I just hope He loves me, too." I knew that I had faith, but growing up in an evangelical mecca like Wheaton, I also knew that being an Episcopalian was considered very cutting edge and possibly heretical.

I knew my dad occasionally worried that he would lose his job at Wheaton College for being an Episcopalian. Along with that, he would joke that his Baptist parents certainly thought we all were "going to hell in a hand basket." I also understood that our heritage was not liturgical and that we had veered off the beaten path from our Baptist missionary and Presbyterian grandparents. Many of our aunts, uncles, and cousins were thoroughly evangelical, too. And I always felt a tension between these worlds. So I perpetually questioned my own faith. As an angst-ridden teen, I was drawn to the sentimental in evangelicalism. I swooned over Amy Grant's songs. I loved reading the psalms at night before bed, or in the middle of the night if I couldn't sleep. I prayed to God, loved Jesus, tried to bless those who were unkind to me, and generally believed that my spiritual life needed attention, direction, and focus.

I tried to be a "good Christian." I also knew I was very far from perfect. I frequently questioned if I was "saved" because I couldn't pinpoint the actual date and hour that I first believed, like so many of my evangelical friends. It took me many years of trying to "feel" saved before I realized that I was being too hard on myself. Of course I was saved. That happened when Jesus died on the cross and when I was baptized into the communion of saints and when I partook of his body and blood, over and over again, growing up. Being saved is something that happens, and it happens again and again. For many years I meditated on the reassurance that "His mercies are new every morning." But it would be a while before I could fully integrate my Episcopalian upbringing with my emerging adult faith, living and learning amongst evangelicals and fundamentalist Christians.

■ ■ ■

Even as I was being molded into a semblance of evangelicalism by my peers and community, there was no doubt that I was drawn to the liturgy. Episcopal worship allowed me to show up with all of my cynicism and angst and woundedness and just "be," stepping into a cosmic event for a brief moment. Every worship service was a chance to be born again. The liturgy, the spoken Word, and the sacraments provided a framework for resting in a timeless line of God's goodness to His people. They gave me a sense of belonging to something so much greater than just myself, or my family, or my community, or the world, but the whole of God's creation, that which exists beyond time. We all showed up as sinners, had the opportunity through the liturgy to confess our faith (however weak at the moment), receive the healing of the Eucharist, and ask for forgiveness, week after week.

That wasn't the message I heard in the evangelical churches and college chapels I attended at the time, which often leaned toward a quick-fix mentality. It was as if I needed just that one prayer or that one moment of insight and I would be washed clean and therefore immediately be less complex and (hopefully) less frustrating to them.

■ ■ ■

Early on, I was surprised to hear that many of my evangelical classmates believed Roman Catholics were not Christians, but pagan. I had to stop in my tracks and furrow my brow. Realizing that Anglicanism was the Catholic church's "stepsister," I feared that I would be rejected by my evangelical friends for not being evangelical enough.

So I initially tried really hard to fit in with the evangelical mindset of those around me. Many of them were wonderful, authentic people with real passion for Jesus. Some were my very best friends, people I loved a lot. But I always felt different. There was a great emphasis on saving souls, on witnessing to people, and that wasn't my gift. I tried to go along, because it seemed that was the litmus test for others as to whether or not I was truly a Christian. I can't say that I ever saved a soul, though.

The summer of 1990, I flew off to an adventure with the Wheaton-in-England program, along with many classmates and several Wheaton professors, which helped to deepen my appreciation for the history of the Church and began to set my mind at ease. We had the chance to visit a popular Anglican church in Oxford, St. Aldates, and I felt the sweet satisfaction of recognition and the awe of worshiping in a place where Christians had been worshiping for a thousand years. I was drawn to the Spirit-filled blend they lived out. The church had the historical rootedness of the liturgy, which tells God's story every week; the evangelical emphasis on personal devotion and spiritual growth; and the charismatic emphasis on the indwelling and outpouring of the Holy Spirit. Together, they expressed a holistic ideal of the narrative of God in the world and in our lives.

We visited many cathedrals. I remember sitting in the gorgeous Canterbury Cathedral with many of my classmates, all of us staring quietly at the unbelievable architecture and absorbing the energy of centuries of history and worship. There is a photo of a group of us, everyone else smiling at the camera except me—my neck is craned and I'm looking straight up at the ceiling. I might have been enraptured by my own personal trail to Canterbury. I certainly loved the connection I felt to my dad's work, this opportunity to understand his dedication and passion. And I felt particularly blessed when my group shared a silent moment and then recited the Lord's Prayer together. That summer I had been praying for healing, and finally in that pilgrimage destination I felt it. It brought back to my heart the experience of reverence and awe before the One who created us and lives in us. It was a moment of mystery and meaning.

I was learning more how to merge my growing sense of being evangelical with my roots of Anglicanism and coming to understand that the challenge was not how to choose between the two, but only how to merge them into a holistic and authentic expression of faith. After I came home from that summer in England, at the age of 21, I decided to be confirmed in the Episcopal Church. There was no doubt in my mind that my faith was deeply rooted in Anglicanism, and I wanted to confess that reality.

■ ■ ■

I met my future husband, Tom, shortly after I returned from England. He was a nice Christian boy from the Reform tradition stronghold of Grand Rapids, Michigan—with a bit of a wild streak. As such, he was perfectly willing to accompany me to my Episcopal Church, and we were married in May 1993 at St. Mark's Episcopal Church.

We moved to Grand Rapids after our wedding and visited several churches, including some Episcopal ones. Ultimately we ended up in Tom's church of origin, a nondenominational Bible church. I never felt at home there, but we had family members and friends there, a built-in community. At that time in our lives, this made sense.

Yet the first time we celebrated the Lord's Supper, hot tears sprang to my eyes and a sense of emptiness gripped me. As I watched the men in black suits file down to the front of the Bible church that Sunday, I thought to myself, "Why is this about the elders? Where is Jesus?" A few words of remembrance were said, and the tiny plastic cups of grape juice were passed around, along with some wafers. "Huh?" I thought. "This is it? Where is the sense of the sacred?" Once again, I found myself struggling. I wanted to fit in with our friends and my new family, but I knew that, for me, something crucial was missing.

Not long after we were married, a friend from Wheaton College moved to Grand Rapids and began preaching at the church we attended. He drew large crowds, and ultimately he started his own church. We followed. Again, it was a crowd of familiar faces, a community of like-minded believers. The preacher challenged us to grow spiritually, and introduced us to a new form of evangelicalism, all of which came as a welcome shift.

The church quickly grew to become a mega-church, drawing 10,000 people to three services each Sunday, moving their location from a large homeschool building to an extra-large abandoned mall. With the growth, it stopped being a familiar community and became a place where we dropped in anonymously and rushed to the parking lot after worship to avoid the huge traffic jam on our way out.

We met great people. I don't regret our years with this church, because it was a season of growth, questioning, challenging ourselves, changing our minds, discovering more about theology, history, the Bible, God, Jesus, and so many things that are crucial to the ongoing life of faith. The cavernous, industrial, theater-in-the-round style church with a magnetic, energetic pastor and rock-band style worship music was simply my resting place for this season of the journey.

Early on, Tom and I made suggestions on how to bring more meaning to the Eucharist, and the leadership listened and tried, with some success, to create a more sacred and meaningful ritual. However, it was difficult to do this with 3,000 people at a time. During some of the years there, the worship team focused on bringing more mystery and contemplation, even some call-and-response liturgy to the worship service. It was always evolving though, so we often weren't surprised to experience an order of worship that was completely different from the week before.

At times, the community and worship were wonderfully charismatic and soul enriching. But slowly, life there began to unravel. First came the changes in leadership and staff; conflict and restructuring dampened our enthusiasm for the church and affected some of our relationships. I often felt the church was floating unanchored, not tied to any authority, and desperately looking for their vision and mission to give them a sense of grounding and roots.

Our kids began to loathe Sunday school because they were in a warehouse-sized room with a hundred other kids their age. The whole place was crowded and noisy. The words of the Wordsworth sonnet echoed in my head: "The world is too much with us." The music began to hurt my ears. I craved more contemplative worship. I was tired of being a passive audience member.

One Sunday I said to my husband Tom, "I'm going to stay out in the hallway, and once the worship time is over, I'll come in and sit with you." The moment those words came out of my mouth, I realized I needed a change. If I needed to get away from worship, well that was the wake-up call. I wasn't worshiping in a way that reflected my deep spiritual needs. I felt ambivalent, unsure where we would go; I only knew I was ready to leave.

Around this time, Tom came home from church on a Sunday that I had stayed home. "How was church?" I asked. He replied, "I think I'm Catholic."

■ ■ ■

Toward the end of our years in that community, my dad died. I think that contributed to my need for more silence and my ambivalence about band- and pastor-centered worship. I became deeply reflective about my dad's work to lead people to a more rooted worship experience, to step into their place in the community of the Creator—which included all the saints who have gone before as a great cloud of witnesses surrounding us and living out God's purposes with us.

As my dad was dying, I asked him to let me know that he was okay once he crossed to the other side. He said he would if he was able, but he wanted me to know that he would always be with me at the Eucharistic table with the communion of saints. I reflected on the many times my dad had prayed with me about things I was struggling with—how he would anoint me with oil and make the sign of the cross on my forehead.

His voice echoed in my head: "Flee to the Eucharist."

In February 2009, on Ash Wednesday, I attended Grace Episcopal Church, just a few minutes' drive from my house. I had been longing for the structure of the church calendar and the liturgy, and I missed practicing Lent. Grief had put me into a state of perpetual Lent most of the time anyway, and I felt the need to plug that into an outlet. I wanted to sit in a hard wooden pew and receive black ashes on my forehead and take the Eucharist with the communion of saints. And so I did.

As I sat there, a feeling of deep peace came to me. I thought to myself, "I'm supposed to be here" and "Maybe this church needs me as much as I need it. Maybe I could be of service here." As Sundays of visiting went by, I picked up on an evangelical thread at Grace Church which felt comfortable to me. I found many friendly and welcoming people, a few Wheaton College connections, and a spirit of authenticity and grace. I discerned a quaint Anglicanism in the rector, and his evangelistic, challenging homilies were a welcome surprise. We were fortunate that a short time after we became members of Grace Church, the church brought on two evangelically minded youth pastors. We were thrilled that our kids would be a part of their vibrant youth group.

I was happy to be back in a "little c" catholic, liturgical church, participating in worship with the familiar words, the emphasis on a broad reading of scripture, the apostolic history, the moments of silence, the reverent singing of the Lord's Prayer, and of course, the Eucharist. Standing, sitting, kneeling, singing, sipping, I was once again absorbing the liturgy into my very being, sensing its sacramental power to heal and transform me on an ongoing basis.

■ ■ ■

Recently, standing atop the ancient city of Rome and lost in thought, I pondered the mysterious trail of the ancient Christian faith and realized what my dad, Robert Webber, had modeled for me: The road to the future runs through the past. Although I don't know where my particular path will lead me, I know that I will always be drawn to the history and mystery of the liturgical church. I am grateful that my husband feels the same way, and that we can share this ancient-future legacy with our children (one of whom attends a Baptist-roots school, while three attend a Catholic school). I hope it will shape them to become more and more like Jesus, as ambassadors of love to a broken world. I hope we can follow—and teach our children—my dad's simple directive: Flee to the Eucharist.

CHAPTER

9

Jon Hall

My introduction to an Anglican style of Holy Week was on Good Friday 2000. It was just after 7:00 p.m. at St. Michael the Archangel Episcopal Church in Lexington, Kentucky. I was there because the Methodist church where I worked as a praise and worship leader didn't have a service planned. A classmate and friend from nearby Asbury Seminary invited me and my wife, Colleen, to join his family for the evening. Take note: that's what Episcopalians do with their friends. Most people invite newcomers to regular Sunday gatherings or Christmas or Easter. Not Episcopalians. They see a stark Good Friday service coming, and they think how much their friends would enjoy it.

We sat near the front. The lights were low and the altar was completely bare. The sanctuary was stripped of every piece of cloth and every vessel from the previous night at the end of the Maundy Thursday service. The combination of silence and dissonant music set the tone for the evening. Then it was time for the proclamation of the Word, which I was hoping to use as a measurement of what this church could really offer. "Here's the test," I thought. "Bring it on, preacher."

The priest stepped from his chair behind the altar. He moved down the steps and positioned himself in front of the congregation. Then, right in front of God Almighty and everybody, he gave a sermon that lasted no more than six or seven minutes. I had just started to settle in for what I thought was the main event when the priest stopped talking and went back to his chair. I thought something must be wrong. I only ever had heard sermons that were approximately thirty to forty minutes. A "homily" might be a scant twenty-five minutes but never anything quicker. Every part of the service revolved around the spoken word. So I was shocked at the priest's brevity. Had he forgotten his sermon notes? I was embarrassed for him.

The focus then shifted to the Altar of Repose and the Reserved Sacrament, which had been consecrated the night before. Every liturgical aspect complemented the one before it and drew me closer to the foot of the cross, which had been placed before us just before communion. The veil of heaven was newly opened. I fell in love with God again that night because the liturgy created a place for me to step into the ancient truth of the Passion narrative.

The sermon that evening was not intended to be the focal point of the liturgy. This was not a preacher- or priest-centered service. Every part of it—including the lights, the quiet, the dissonance, the stripped-down delivery of the homily—unselfishly and effectively ushered us to contemplate the cross and our relationship to it. It was in that service that I learned "even if the sermon stinks, you still get Jesus," as a friend once said. The same would prove to be true of every Eucharist since then.

■ ■ ■

I left that service thinking of people with whom I wanted to share my experience. "People need to know that Holy Week services are more than pit stops to Easter morning," I thought. I had stumbled into an ancient-future conversation and wanted to share it with my family and my congregation.

I was, at that point in 1999–2000, a student at Asbury Theological Seminary in Wilmore, Kentucky, and a praise and worship leader at a United Methodist church in Lexington. That church was trying on a more nondenominational and seeker-oriented approach by moving away from the liturgical calendar. We had sermon series that loosely followed the lectionary cycle, but most Sunday mornings were thematically up for grabs depending on the topic of the month.

And yet, as the praise leader I sensed a hunger in the congregation for a liturgical connection to their lives. I was beginning to see how liturgy shapes the rest of our lives. Piecemeal sermon series throughout the year and selecting music and prayers that pointed toward the sermon and the day's theme were all proving to have a short shelf life. I wondered how the congregation would respond to more liturgical worship. And so I pondered:

What if the sermon and everything that surrounded it yielded so that people could partake of Christ crucified and resurrected every week?

Would they want Holy Communion more than once a month sitting in the pews?

Would they participate by kneeling or standing?

I believed there was more to offer. However, as time ran on, I felt more like a jazz artist who had awakened on a marching band bus. The worship team, with a nod from the pastor, designed a couple of services that were based on serving Eucharist. Everything pointed toward communion with God and with one another. When people were offered the chance to come forward for communion, they cried. They were praying with their whole selves before the altar table.

■ ■ ■

About the same time, I attended a Robert Webber workshop in Lexington at another United Methodist church. It was there that I heard Webber's explanation of the Eucharistic elements of bread and wine and experienced the invitation to reflect more deeply on my spiritual home. As he held up bread and wine, elevating it in an Instructional Eucharist style, he said something like, "Serving stingy communion elements communicates we believe in a stingy God. God is not stingy and neither should we be." That image blazed part of my Canterbury Trail, and his words ring true for me today as I plan sacramental worship that, at its best, fills all the senses with the wonderful abundance of God. This abundance comes alive in the preparation of the elements themselves, but also in the frequency with which we celebrate Holy Communion. I began to think, "If Communion, in all of its incarnations, is a daily offering for relationship with our God, then it can certainly be celebrated as a weekly one."

I had also just read the first edition of *Evangelicals on the Canterbury Trail*. The book surprised me with its combination of evangelical fortitude and liturgical sensibilities. It brought tears to my eyes. I realized that my evangelical Wesleyan identity was shifting to a new expression of faith, one linked to a rich Anglican tradition. Like desiring ancient water that is purified after filtering through layers of rock, I found myself thirsty for the full liturgy of the Church from the deepest wells.

Up to this point I had not put these experiences in the context of changing denominations. I was thinking of them more as a subtle shift into reclaiming my Wesleyan Methodist roots in daily prayer and more frequent communion. I was also deeply invested in my discernment process; I had moved with my wife to attend seminary two years earlier. I was on a track to finish that course of study the following year and return to the house we owned in the Texas hill country. Our plans were to return to that home, pay our dues in the itinerancy by accepting pastoral appointments, and then live out our days in bliss in the original neighborhood. However, the one day I had not counted on was that Good Friday in 2000.

I remember feeling joyous and calling my parents to tell them I was attending a church that I was really excited about. I told them about the Good Friday service and that there was another service that I also thought was incredible called the Easter Vigil (an extended service of multiple Bible readings, ancient prayers, songs, and baptisms to anticipate celebrating the resurrection of Christ). They had never heard of an Easter Vigil celebration or the *Book of Common Prayer*. My new enthusiasm was only met with resistance. When I told them I was studying about our roots in Anglicanism, attending worship, and considering changing denominations, there was a thick silence. My mother asked, "Why are you rejecting the Methodist church?" Then it was my turn to pause for a moment. "Well, I don't think I am," I said. "I still relate to Methodist roots, but I'm not sure where they are going."

It was getting harder to recognize and interpret the traditions of the church I had always known. The tenets of Methodism such as John Wesley's Quadrilateral (Scripture, Tradition, Experience, and Reason), which I had grown up studying and later teaching in confirmation classes, were taking on a new life. I could see them lived out in the Episcopal Church with an emphasis on morning and evening prayer, weekly communion, and a community gathered around cycles of worship.

It was quite a journey to go through a Methodist college and the better part of two years of seminary, thinking I knew our tradition only to find out in a history class that the Wesley brothers, John and Charles, were Anglicans. I liken it to discovering as a child in Vacation Bible School that Jesus was raised in a good Jewish family.

John and Charles Wesley, in their respective contexts, utilized the theology of the church fathers, studied the scriptures in their original languages, and practiced the means of grace, including frequent Holy Communion as a regular spiritual discipline. I remember wanting to connect to as much of that living history as possible. I wanted to know how the perspective of Jesus, the early church apostles, the men and women of faith through the centuries of the church, and the Christian family tree, both Protestant and Catholic, were being manifested in current faith contexts.

■ ■ ■

I understood the new ground I was treading was unsettling for my parents. My mother's side of the family included five Methodist pastors. I was expected to be the next one. We never said it that plainly, but we didn't have to. I needed to figure out how I was being called, whether it was as clergy or a lay leader. The Methodist part was a given.

My grandmother, who spent a great deal of time researching the family's genealogy, was fond of saying that our family of origin was "good Methodists." Other kids on our street and at school were Italian, Irish, African-American, German, Jewish, or Hispanic. Everybody else seemed to have at least one country, somewhere, to call home. But in our family, being Methodist was its own kind of "home country."

She has since passed away, and I have come to appreciate her pride in our family history. I have also come to realize that "home" can be a state of mind or a posture of our hearts. The Holy Spirit continually points us to our spiritual Zions. As some cultures turn their bodies and kneel towards their homeland, I think she was speaking the same thing in terms of her faith. I understood it. I had just come to the point where to fulfill being a "good Methodist" meant returning to an Anglican foundation.

On the one hand, I believed my family was supportive. I think they could hear in my voice a genuine connection with my new church. However, I could tell our reference points were diverging. I grieve that our faith lives have continued to be distant. Similarly, I felt a divergence with some of my seminary friends who also were attracted to Anglicanism, but not the Episcopal Church itself. I had about 20 friends and classmates who went that direction while my wife and I stayed within the Episcopal Church. Issues of sexuality, the authority of bishops, and property rights became regular conversations, as we increasingly grew apart. The lost friendships were a heavy price to pay for staying in the Episcopal Church. I trusted we were all intent on being true to God's calling, but the interpretations of scripture and reason were never going to be identical among us.

■ ■ ■

It was late in 2001, as a Master's in Counseling student at Asbury, that I began to consider a second discernment process, this time in the Episcopal Church. I was in an intern counseling session with a client whose crisis centered on being shunned by a congregation. The only way I was allowed to address spiritual topics was if the client brought them up first *and* we limited ourselves to the specific issue at hand. I remember thinking that all the textbooks and counseling theories were not going to draw out a solution. This person also needed healing within a healthy community.

Later that day, I was in the Wednesday evening Eucharist with at least a dozen other worshipers. When the priest served Communion, I thought about the gift I was receiving and what it meant to be there with other pilgrims. I thought about the meeting with the client just a few hours earlier and wondered what level of estrangement the client might be dealing with at the same moment. I watched the evening light stream through the windows and across the sanctuary and thought, "If my client could experience this worship, at least it would be a start." The Church can be used to curse or to bless one another, to bind or to loose. I think taking Communion reminds us of whose we are and what we are becoming. We figure out faith together based on an economy of God's grace, which is open for everyone.

The synergy of God's use of grace and timing has come to me many times since. I remember the knock on the door in 2003 from a teenager whose parents had just kicked her out. With tears streaming down both cheeks, the teenager said that, even though she did not know me, she had known something about the graciousness of the Episcopal Church. But she didn't want me; she wanted Jesus. My job was to be faithful to the timing God had orchestrated. It was to play the song of God's grace live, directly with people.

■ ■ ■

God's timing dances in and around our superficial agendas, and in this church, I have learned to open and participate in that mysterious dance. There was the Saturday I was standing in the parking lot of the local hardware store in Harrodsburg, Kentucky. I had been the Episcopal pastor for three years and knew many people in town. I was talking to a complete stranger who serendipitously pulled up with an empty truck next to me as I was unsuccessfully trying to tie an extension ladder to the roof of my Honda.

It was Advent of 2008, and St. Philip's Episcopal Church was putting up decorations after the last service before Christmas Eve. People in the town had known our pre-Civil War church for its architecture and the beauty of its Christmas Eve service. We had also started a monthly community meal ministry that started out small but was now serving 250–300 meals on a single night, enlisting several congregations, agencies, and volunteers who weren't members of any church.

As we loaded the ladder into his truck bed, he kindly asked where he was going to take it. "Is your church the one that has the daycare?" "No," I said. "That's the Baptist church." He continued, "Are you the church with the big doors at the top of the steps?" "No. That's the Christian church," I said. His eyebrows were now at varying latitudes. Then he looked me straight in the eye, smiled, and said, "Oh, you're the church that feeds people." "Yes," I said, "We are the church that feeds people."

He had our ladder in his truck. He knew where to go because we fed people.

Sometimes when I think about meetings and liturgies and the details of my best-laid plans for the church, I remember what it is all about. Whether it is a Good Friday service at the invitation of a friend, a knock on the front door by a stranger, or a hot dinner inside a to-go box, true worship that continually shapes our lives is ultimately about paying attention so that God's people are indeed fed.

Let everything that has breath praise the Lord!

CHAPTER

10

David Madeira

My journey from evangelicalism to Anglicanism may best begin with a biblical paraphrase (my apologies to St. Paul in Philippians 3): If any has reason to be confident in his evangelical upbringing, I have more. Raised in Wheaton, Illinois, arguably the heart of American evangelicalism, and descended from a lineage of Wheaton College graduates (all of my grandparents attended Wheaton and remained lifelong friends with Billy and Ruth Graham, and my parents, aunts, uncles, and cousins are alums as well, and my father was even an administrator there for a time), I grew up immersed in scripture, hearing long, doctrinal sermons before I could wrap my head around them. I could spout off fundamental Christian teaching, explain to others the tenets of the faith, and knew from a very early age the wonderful truth about Jesus. Immersed in evangelical Christianity from the beginning, I have believed in Jesus for as long as I can remember.

But until I experienced liturgy, I hadn't the faintest clue of what it meant to worship him.

■ ■ ■

My journey on the Canterbury Trail begins with my parents' divorce when I was around seven years old. My family had been attending a renowned evangelical church in Wheaton, and my mom continued to do so after their split. But my dad began to attend an Episcopal church in Geneva, Illinois. Alternating weekends with my parents meant going back and forth between these two liturgical styles, and without really knowing what was happening, I had the rare opportunity to engage in long comparative analysis of the evangelical and Episcopal traditions during my grade-school years. Though their differences didn't register with me as much more than stylistic at the time, this comparative study planted seeds in me that would continue to grow throughout my adolescence and early adulthood. Over the years, the theological and doxological significance of these traditions became more and more clear, and those years straddling two traditions are undoubtedly a major reason why I am a doctoral student in the study of worship today.

Now with the opportunity to reflect on these early years with a more mature mind, I am a little more able to describe what it was about the Episcopal Church that planted the seeds of liturgical worship in me. As I write this, I imagine going back in time and conducting an interview with the child of my youth. What would I have said (if asked then) appealed to me about Anglicanism, and how do I interpret that today?

I'm sure one of the ways I would have described the appeal of my dad's church was that the liturgy was much more engaging, far beyond mere sitting and listening. One of the primary differences between these churches was that, while my mom's evangelical church engaged my intellect, my dad's church called for an expression of worship that involved my whole body as well as my mind. The evangelical service was dominated by a lengthy, heady sermon, and the pastor was revered for his extensive study and theological prowess. I don't for a second wish to diminish the importance of solid preaching, and I am very grateful that I grew up hearing the Word of God taught with conviction and strong doctrine. However, that church seemed to do little more than put deep, fascinating truths in my head, and that was if my young attention span could make it all the way through the sermon.

At Dad's church my whole being was engaged. We spent time on our knees praying both corporate prayers and individual ones during times of reflection. We heard four passages of scripture every Sunday, one of which (the Psalm) we sang together, engaging our voices with the Word of God. On high and holy days, the room was filled with the fragrance of incense; we watched as the smoke billowed from the censers and ascended high to the ceiling, representing the ascent of our prayers to God the Father. Most important was the time we knelt at the Communion rail, felt the bread of Christ's body pressed into our palms, and then placed it on our tongues, followed by a sip of wine from the cup of Christ. All five of our senses were engaged.

As a kid, all I probably knew was that this was simply a more interesting way to worship. As an adult I consider more deeply the implication of this multi-sensory dialogue with God. Those evangelical traditions steeped in post-Enlightenment rationalism have long divorced the intellect from the flesh. It matters little what the body does in worship, as long as the mind understands. In fact, it may be even more important to disengage the body so that it does not interfere with the affairs of the mind. Therefore, the service at my mom's church was almost entirely focused on hearing and understanding, and there emerged a rift between my mind and my body, almost as if it didn't really matter what my body was doing as long as my mind believed the right things. Was some of my high school and college behavior, which didn't strike me as incongruous with my Christian faith, a product of the fact that I spent so much time in a church that engaged only my mind? That church, in fact, did teach the importance of good moral behavior, but without actually engaging my body in any way, did I miss what should have been an obvious connection between belief and behavior? If, as I was taught, my body is a temple, why did it go unused in worship after being parked in a pew?

The intellectualization of spirituality at Mom's evangelical church paved the way for me to appreciate the sacramentality at Dad's Episcopal congregation. As a child I might have described the Episcopal Church as more "mystical" or more "holy." What I was experiencing for the first time was a tradition that cherishes sacramentality and doesn't attempt to bring every aspect of God's saving grace under the umbrella of human reason. At the evangelical church, transformation occurred inside your mind. If you could understand the sermon, it might move you to a new kind of understanding that had some sort of moral implication.

Again, I don't want to sound overly critical of intellectualism; these were brilliant, deeply learned pastors from whom I learned a great deal about the Christian faith, and reading theology remains a pleasure of mine today. But what I had no sense of until I began to attend a liturgical church every other weekend was that a relationship with the Triune God is filled with heavenly mysteries, and that it is more important to engage with those mysteries than to be able to explain them. After all, the point is that God is the one at work, engaging us, regardless of our ability to understand what he is doing.

In the Episcopal Church the sermon was a small part of a much larger ceremony, and that ceremony was filled with a sense that God was acting out a cosmic plan of redemption and re-creation. We had been invited to participate in that story. Some of it we can understand, and some of it we will never grasp, but the dialogue between God and humans in worship transcends right doctrine; it engages and transforms far more than the intellect. It is a divine mystery into which we are invited, whether or not we are graced with the power to understand it fully. The power of God to re-create the world is not limited to that which humans can understand and explain.

■ ■ ■

Mom's church felt like no place for sinners; Dad's church was populated by them. At the evangelical church I felt like everybody was so perfectly put together and I needed to be as well. If I was good enough, like our revered pastor, I would be a good-standing member in God's family. We went to Mom's church on our best behavior, looking our "Sunday best," because God forbid you would reveal an imperfect charac-ter there in the sight of all those saints. The great irony was that I went to that church looking and acting my best, and left feeling my worst. At Dad's church, I went a sinner, and having partaken in a whole liturgy of heavenly mysteries, I left feeling intimately loved and redeemed by God, because he had welcomed me at his table despite my sinfulness.

It's not that the evangelical church preached a doctrine of "works righteousness" or "cheap grace." Mom's church had (and has) great, solid preaching on a Christian, biblical understanding of salvation. It's just that this was all so internal. Even though you learned that you and everyone around you was a sinner and in need of God's love, nobody around you looked like sinners because you never saw what was going on inside of anyone. Well, that's the problem: It was all inside. Nobody was kneeling before the cross confessing their sins in the sight of God and their neighbors. Other than the line "forgive us our debts" in the Lord's Prayer, there was never even any real confession of sin. We acted sinless and never acknowledged that we could be anything else than that. I knew I was sinful but hoped nobody noticed. We sat, listened, learned, and continued to look our best. And I felt my worst.

At the Episcopal church it was a much different story, but it wasn't the preaching or the attitude of the congregation that made the difference. There, expressed through the liturgy and its corporate nature, I was a sinner in a sea of sinners. Lay people around me and clergy in front of me all knelt before the cross, confessed their sins, and received God's free gift of forgiveness at the Eucharist. It's one thing to hear a pastor preach that "all have sinned and fall short of the glory of God"; it's quite another thing to see him and everyone around you kneeling before the cross, asking for forgiveness. At Mom's church I felt unworthy to be in the presence of God and hear about his mercy; at Dad's church I felt the wideness of his mercy because I and everyone around me was acknowledging together that we were unworthy of his love.

■ ■ ■

What this discussion boils down to is that the evangelical church taught me to believe in Jesus, but the Episcopal Church showed me how to worship him. In all honesty I am very thankful that I had both as I grew up, but at some point I eventually had to choose whether church was for learning about God or corporately falling before him as Lord. In the evangelical church we met, sang a hymn, said the Apostle's Creed, and heard scripture and a choral anthem, but then the rest of the service was dominated by the pastoral prayer and sermon. After the sermon there was a short time of quiet reflection before the postlude kicked in and we were dismissed. However, with the exception of the hymn and creed, we sat still and listened to everything. We did not go through any actions of actual worship, and so I never even imagined that the Christian faith could go any deeper than understanding and believing what the Bible said about Christ.

The liturgy taught me how to go beyond belief into worship. The actions of liturgy—the opening acclamations, singing of Psalms, reading of scripture, confession of sin, intercessory prayer, celebration of the Eucharist, and everything else contained therein—point beyond mere believing the story and direct us to full engagement, individually and corporately, in the worship of the Triune God.

Finally, I believe the liturgy engages scripture differently than the evangelical tradition in which I was raised, despite the skilled exegesis found in the preaching of the latter. In Mom's church, there would be long sermon series on books of the Bible, usually epistles. Someone would read maybe two or three verses and then the preacher would systematically "unpack" the text word by word for forty-five minutes. If you could pay attention that long, I'm sure you learned something pretty profound, but to me it sounded more like the literary criticism papers I would later write in high school.

In the Episcopal liturgy of my dad's church, scripture seemed to be allowed to speak more for itself, and the story of God from the beginning to the end of time was presented in a much more holistic way, allowing us to find our place in the story. At Episcopal worship we had at least four biblical passages—Old Testament, Psalm, epistle, and gospel—read every Sunday. They were usually all connected by a similar theme. This theme was explained more in depth in the sermon, and we were given a picture of how things that God revealed to Israel (Old Testament reading) became a part of its spiritual and prophetic consciousness (Psalm), and then were fulfilled and recapitulated in Christ (gospel) as interpreted in the New Testament (epistle). It wasn't about extricating every morsel of meaning from something Paul wrote; it was about how the mysteries of God have been progressively revealed from the beginning to the end, all pointing to Christ.

Furthermore, the liturgy culminates in something without which, at least for me, there is a huge hole: the Eucharist—a mysterious, sacramental, corporate response where the holy Lord who has just been revealed through his Word now extends an invitation to all people to join him at his table.

Whether we can ever fully comprehend the mechanisms of our salvation, the opportunity to commune with the Lord of hosts in the fellowship of all believers is extended to us every time we join together in worship. In an unfathomable, cosmic mystery, the master narrative from everlasting to everlasting converges with the finite here and now; we find ourselves in the story of God through the sacramental signs of infinite and abundant grace.

Of course, I couldn't articulate any of this as a child. There was just something special about Sundays congregated with other worshipers in this small Episcopal church in Geneva, Illinois.

■ ■ ■

I continued to alternate churches until my high school years. In my last few years before college, my dad took another job that required him to travel quite often, leaving him unable to regularly attend church. But when I finally had my own car and the freedom to choose where to worship, I began making the drive a few towns over to Geneva on the weekends. I didn't really know anybody; my semi-regular attendance and my dad's penchant for anonymity meant we hadn't made many church friends. I was fine with that at the time, however, because after the feeling of being the only sinner in a room of saints at my mom's church, it was refreshing to feel anonymous in, yet completely unified with, a body of worshipers, many of whom probably felt the same way I did.

In the fall after graduation, I moved to Nashville, Tennessee to begin studies in music at Belmont University, a small, Christian, liberal arts college with Baptist roots. I didn't have a car at first, so my church attendance was governed by friends; I hitched rides with whomever I could. In the Bible Belt, this led me to quite a few Baptist churches. I also attended a contemporary non-denominational evangelical church that was popular with the college students of the area, but when a recurring problem emerged—they couldn't start the service until everyone made it through the coffee line—I decided I needed a little more reverence and ceremony.

In the meantime, I began to suffer a crisis of faith, asking questions like, "Why do I believe what I believe? Is it because I was brought up this way, or do I really believe it?" At this time my spiritual formation was still more built upon the doctrinal theology of my mom's evangelical church, and the appeals of the liturgical church I have expressed above were little more than feelings far beneath the surface. But I recognize now that I was no longer able to build my house upon theology and doctrine alone. I was looking to declare allegiance to something, to engage fully my mind and my body in worship of the Trinity.

My uncle, a Nashville-based musician, introduced me to St. Bartholomew's Episcopal Church, which he had been attending for a few years. I began to attend semi-regularly in my last year of college, but I also slept in more Sunday mornings than I'd like to admit. St. Bartholomew's was under the leadership of an interim pastor, but a few things stuck out to me under this temporary leadership.

First, the interim pastor was a woman. I'm not sure I had ever heard a woman preach. At my mom's evangelical church, women are not only unable to preach, but are also not able to serve as elders. The interim rector at St. Bartholomew's, however, preached the gospel in a way that I'd never heard before. With feeling and conviction, she pointed worshipers in all walks of life simply to the cross of Jesus, with heartfelt confidence in the powerful name of Christ to penetrate the darkest corners of our souls.

Second, St. Bartholomew's was the most welcoming church I had ever attended. I had been to churches where no one bothered to extend a hand all morning, and I'd been to churches where you get so smothered with welcomes that it feels like people are just trying to meet some greeting quota as quickly as possible. But at St. Bartholomew's, Sunday after Sunday I was met by authentically smiling faces, thrilled to know who I was, and who remembered me on the Sundays when I returned. Nobody dragged me off somewhere to get me "plugged in." They just seemed genuinely happy to have met another brother in God's family.

That fall after graduation, I moved in with my uncle for the better part of the next year. St. Bartholomew's was under new leadership and was undergoing its own period of rediscovery. With no one begging me to get involved, I acclimated to what I would come to call my church home, and eventually I began to participate as a volunteer musician once a month. Relationships developed, friendships were made, and for the first time I learned what it meant to have a "church family," to wake up on Sunday mornings with not an obligation but an actual desire to worship the Lord in his temple, and to want more of a role in the church's activities, not less.

Having returned to a liturgical church with new eyes and a more mature mind, the liturgy opened doors and windows to worship that I was only beginning to understand. I learned to fully appreciate the beauty of written, corporate prayer. I learned to view liturgy as a platform, not as the object of worship itself, but as a means by which we are brought into the presence of God, where his story is proclaimed and enacted, from creation to re-creation, and where we join with the hosts of heaven in praising the Triune God of heaven and earth.

When I began dating a girl named Elizabeth the next year, I was worried that she might not feel the way that I did about the liturgical church, having been raised in a Baptist church. I feared she would not be comfortable with liturgy, that she would have been taught "a read prayer is a dead prayer," and that we would have to begin church shopping together until we found a place we could both tolerate. However, in those first Sundays at St. Bartholomew's I was thrilled to see Elizabeth opening to a whole new expression of faith. She was engaging with her whole being more deeply than she had in any church before. We were married at St. Bartholomew's a year and a half later and are about to baptize our first child there.

■ ■ ■

Over the course of the next few years, my role increased at St. Bartholomew's, and I now have the honor of serving as its associate director of music, directing a choir of some of the most generous, loving, humble people I have ever met. Now, on the other side of the planning of worship, I am humbled by the opportunity to help craft worship services, and to revisit memories of what I learned growing up straddling two different traditions.

I must make clear before ending that I have a great appreciation and affinity for the evangelical church in which I was brought up before I was exposed to Anglicanism. There was and is a theological depth to the sermons preached there that I have rarely encountered elsewhere. I did not encounter bad teaching there, nor was I ever treated in an unkind manner by anyone at the church. My mom's church has one of the best, most active and influential missions ministries I have ever seen, a wonderful children's Sunday school program, and a disabilities ministry that has enabled dozens of families to experience community and church fellowship in ways they had never before imagined. And yet, I believe, those ministries arise naturally from that very rational, post-Enlightenment strain of Protestantism that de-emphasizes the mysteries of God, the full-bodied nature of worship, the profound significance of the Eucharist, and many other features of liturgical and historic Christianity. While I was brought up with a strong belief in Jesus, I hadn't the faintest clue of what it meant to worship him.

I certainly don't have it all figured out today, nor do I think the Episcopal Church, or liturgical traditions in general, are without their weaknesses. However, experiencing and engaging God through liturgy may have saved my faith when intellectual doctrine seemed unable to effect meaningful transformation in my life. I am thankful for the many flavors of Christian faith expressed worldwide today, but I know it was God's grace that put me on this transformational journey down the Canterbury Trail.

CHAPTER

11

Linda and Bill Richardson

Most people think Southern California is a stronghold of religious and political liberalism. That might be true in Hollywood, but in most evangelical churches in Southern California in the 1960s and '70s, a widespread conservatism was the order of the day. That included a deep distrust of all mainline denominations and their particular expressions of Christianity. That distrust was passed onto us having roots in a conservative Baptist church and being shaped early on in that tradition. So when our perspectives began to change from a free-church orientation to a liturgical one, it was a radical departure from all that most around us held dear. The story of how that happened is truly *our* story, so we're going to tell it together.

• • •

Linda: I was raised in a Christian home and faithfully attended a conservative Baptist church through high school, having received Jesus into my life at about age five and having been baptized by immersion at ten. Upon entering college in 1961, I joined a sorority and promptly put my faith on a shelf and stopped attending church. Bill and I had known one another in high school, but began dating seriously late in our sophomore year in college.

Bill: I grew up in a loving, stable though unchurched home. At age 19, I found the Lord at a Billy Graham Crusade in Los Angeles, and began attending the Baptist church that my girlfriend and future wife, Linda, had attended as a child. At the time, we were both students at California State University in Long Beach; the year was 1963.

Linda: My parents had insisted I invite Bill to hear Billy Graham and, when he surprisingly responded to the invitation that evening, I had a conflicted reaction. I liked my life as it was, and was concerned that Bill's newfound faith was going to radically change things. I reluctantly returned to my church with him, and we graduated from college and were married in June 1965.

Around 1967, through the influence of Campus Crusade for Christ, we attended a Leadership Training Institute. That weekend we were introduced to the ministry of the Holy Spirit, and I experienced a spiritual awakening that pushed me to seek a deeper walk with God. Shortly thereafter, we were asked to partner with our friends, Ken and Martha, to sponsor the high school youth group at our Baptist church.

Bill was teaching science in a local high school and coaching baseball. I was working as a speech and language therapist, and in that context I met two older women who were deeply committed to Jesus and who I greatly respected. We started meeting at lunch once a week, and over the next couple of years I read books like A.W. Tozer's *The Pursuit of God* and Brother Lawrence's *The Practice of the Presence of God.*

Each evening as I waited for Bill to get home from baseball practice, I listened to an Episcopal priest named Dennis Bennett on the radio. Father Bennett was involved in the charismatic renewal going on at that time. His blend of passion for God and thoughtful Christianity was very appealing, and my hunger for a deeper spirituality increased.

During that time Bill and Ken (who worked at IBM) both began to consider leaving their secular positions to train for full-time ministry. Martha and I met each Friday morning for prayer and we prayed that our husbands would, in fact, enter seminary. These prayers were expressions of the call toward ministry that Martha and I felt, but, at the time and in our context, a married woman going to seminary was not an option. Within a year both Ken and Bill did resign their positions and begin seminary.

Bill: Following my conversion, I grew as a new believer through the good teaching and mentoring in our church. As I taught high school and coached baseball, I gradually felt the call of God on my life toward full-time ministry. That culminated the evening my school won the Southern California varsity baseball championship. I sensed the Lord asking me if I wanted to give my life to baseball or to ministry. It was 1970 and the next week I resigned from my teaching and coaching position and in September entered Talbot Seminary in La Mirada, California. That summer our first son was born.

Linda: Martha and I attended BSF (Bible Study Fellowship). As we studied the Gospel of Matthew, Jenny, a woman in my discussion group, shared her perspective about the Lord's Supper; her thoughtful consideration of the topic challenged me and I asked her some questions. I discovered she was Roman Catholic, and she gave me a book of Catholic doctrine to read. What I read directly challenged the view that I had been taught, that the Lord's Supper was simply a remembrance of what Jesus had done on the cross. Through my reading and conversations with Jenny, my heart and mind opened to the possibility of other views of communion.

That led me to do a personal study from scripture that was really quite simple. I took a yellow tablet and drew a line down the center. One side was titled "A remembrance" and the other side "More." I proceeded to read through the New Testament; on the left I listed scriptures that pointed to communion being simply a remembrance, and on the right I wrote down those scriptures that seemed to indicate that communion was "more." I had only two scriptures listed on the left side and a full column on the right. It was the beginning of a shift in my thinking about the Lord's Supper toward a more sacramental view, though I didn't have those words to describe what was happening.

Bill: While attending seminary I served as college pastor at our Baptist church and was exposed to the revival taking place among young people in Southern California. I began to read about churches of all persuasions that were experiencing a true renewal in worship and outreach, but both at our church and at seminary the mainline Christian churches such as the United Methodists, Presbyterians, American Baptists, and Episcopalians were considered "liberal" and were functionally ignored. They were not considered orthodox, and those that were liturgical were seen to simply be "going through the motions" of a stiff and formal religion.

Linda: In February of 1970, I went to St. James by the Sea Episcopal Church in Newport Beach (it was the first time I'd been in an Episcopal church) to hear Father Dennis and Rita Bennett speak. It was a powerful evening, and the Holy Spirit touched me in a significant way that evening and the softening of my attitude toward mainline Christians continued.

Bill: Because we loved college students and had been working with them for three years at our church, following seminary I was appointed as a campus minister with our denomination's home mission society. In 1975, our second son was born and we moved to the Midwest to begin a ministry at Ferris State College in Big Rapids, Michigan. During our five years at Ferris, our college group flourished. During this time I became a part of the campus ministers' fellowship that included campus pastors from many Christian denominations, and my association with them began to break down my prejudices against mainline churches. I realized that these men and women loved Jesus and expressed that love powerfully, though most of them didn't use evangelical vocabulary in articulating their faith.

Gradually our hearts turned toward pastoral ministry because of our interest in worship renewal and a desire to have more long-term input into peoples' lives. In April of 1980, we left Big Rapids and moved to Glen Ellyn, Illinois, where I became the pastor of a small, wounded congregation that was very open to worship renewal.

Coming to First Baptist Church of Glen Ellyn meant that we began to meet people who had been influenced by Dr. Robert

Webber, then a professor at nearby Wheaton College. One of those people was our choir director, Randy Peterson, a recent Wheaton graduate. Randy became a part of our worship committee at First Baptist; together we planned each worship service.

At Easter of 1981, Randy encouraged us to accompany him to an Easter Vigil service at St. Barnabas Episcopal Church in Glen Ellyn. We were nervous—a bit intimidated—but excited nonetheless. That the service was to begin at 10:30 p.m. was only the first shock. As we entered the church, the stillness was profound. (The moments preceding worship in Baptist churches are generally a time for congregants to gather socially.) Besides being quiet, the sanctuary was crowded and the congregation was generationally diverse. Though the service was formal and "high" (bells and smells), the priest was warm and informal at times. The blend of formality and informality surprised us.

A deacon entered the darkened church from the back, carrying a huge lit candle, and sang, "The light of Christ." The congregation responded, "Thanks be to God." The light in the darkness and the words sung penetrated our souls. The liturgy was beautifully chanted—a stretch for us—and large portions of scripture were read aloud for more than an hour, all in relative darkness. We were juggling the order of worship, the *Book of Common Prayer*, a traditional hymnal (with liturgical music and hymns in different sections), and a contemporary music book. Add to that the small candle we were given upon entering the church, and we were getting a full initiation to liturgical worship.

After an hour or more of darkness and shortly after midnight, the priest stood and shouted, "Alleluia! Christ is risen!" The lights came up and the congregation responded immediately and loudly, "The Lord is risen indeed! Alleluia!" We personally missed shouting the acclamation because we were so busy looking for our place in the prayer book, but we didn't miss the power of the words. The place was filled with a level of joy that we had rarely experienced in any church before. The Great Vigil of Easter was now erasing the stereotypes we had in our minds of liturgical worship. The service proceeded with baptisms and the Eucharist, and at every point we were at attention, taking in the sights and sounds.

As we drove home that night, we were first silent and then expressed amazement. We had both appreciated the service and realized that God was opening our hearts to a historic dimension of worship and a different expression of his body. That service set us firmly on the Canterbury Trail even though we remained Baptist for twelve more years. During those years, inspired by our experience and led by the Holy Spirit, we experimented with a variety of worship forms. As Baptists do, we took communion only once a month, but we often imported large sections of the Eucharistic liturgy from the *Book of Common Prayer* and gradually moved further toward the conviction that communion was much more than a remembrance, as we had been taught and long believed.

Between 1981 and 1993, when on vacation we always attended Episcopal churches, and Linda went to St. Mark's Episcopal Church in Glen Ellyn for special services and conferences. Our hearts and minds were moving gradually but steadily in the direction of a more historic and liturgical expression of our faith. Basically, every chance we got, we tried to stay connected to this exciting "new but old" expression of faith. We privately called ourselves "closet Episcopalians."

During these years we read a number of books by Robert "Bob" Webber and we had the opportunity of having several personal conversations with him. His journey from Protestant fundamentalism into the Episcopal Church encouraged us and validated our journey on the Canterbury Trail. Learning the history of the Episcopal liturgy impacted us deeply as we realized its ancient roots. We learned that some parts went back to the earliest centuries of the Church. Our congregation at the Baptist church began to feel the impact of our movement toward liturgical worship. While they were very patient and open to our journey, it was clear that most in the congregation and leadership were not moving in the same direction.

By 1993, we realized our theology was shifting and our hearts were leaning more and more in the liturgical, Episcopal direction. After years of prayer and soul searching, in March of 1993 I resigned as pastor of First Baptist of Glen Ellyn and we began to look for an Episcopal church to attend.

We found Church of the Resurrection which met in Wheaton, and there we encountered for the first time a blend of evangelical commitment to scripture, the ancient contemplative liturgy, and a charismatic openness to the Holy Spirit. For at least six weeks, we wept in every service because we felt we had come home to where our hearts had been leading us for years. I had no job, we didn't know what was next, but we were home.

Shortly thereafter on a trip to Nashville, we read aloud to one another from Robert Webber's book *Evangelicals on the*

Canterbury Trail. We laughed and cried as we read the stories of others who had walked a similar path, and they gave us words to describe what we were feeling. We thanked God as we clarified for ourselves the things that attracted us to the liturgical church:

- the long history of the liturgy;
- the recitation of the creeds and the power of those words;
- the opportunity in the liturgy for participation of the people;
- the blend of evangelical, liturgical, and charismatic;
- the importance of symbols and the liturgical seasons;
- the emphasis on the Word of God read aloud and, at the same time, the de-centralization of the sermon;
- the de-emphasis on personality-centered ministry;
- the elevation of the Table and the real presence of Jesus in the weekly observance of the Eucharist; and
- belief that in the sacraments God is supernaturally present.

(We continued to wrestle with infant baptism and, to this day, find this is the greatest hurdle that free-church people wrestle with as they move along the Canterbury Trail.)

Soon after, a very disturbing thing happened. Church of the Resurrection announced they would be leaving the Episcopal Church USA (now known simply as the Episcopal Church). We were confused. Why the departure from ECUSA? We were told the issue that was causing the parish to leave was a difference in the view of the authority of scripture and its use in ordering the life of individuals and the Church. Though we respected the leaders at Resurrection, we also realized there were evangelical believers in several other local Episcopal churches whose parishes were choosing to stay in ECUSA to be orthodox voices from within. The announced move had a great impact on us personally, as Linda and I had begun to meet with the parish discernment committee, the first step in the process of moving toward ordination to the Episcopal priesthood.

We had a decision to make: would we remain at Church of the Resurrection or would we move to an Episcopal church to follow that path for my ordination? We realized that if we stayed at Resurrection, our options for pastoral ministry would be quite limited with no larger connection to other churches.

Linda: After much prayer and soul searching, we decided to stay with Church of the Resurrection as it left, because of the sense of joy and comfort we had from our relationships in this parish and from the way it combined beautifully the three streams of Christianity that had become so important to us. Practically, that meant that Bill would have to find employment outside of pastoral ministry for a time and I would need to continue to work full time. I kept that commitment, but I also completed a two-year training program in the ancient art of spiritual direction and I began to offer spiritual direction from our home.

Bill: We plunged into ministry at Church of the Resurrection, now an "independent Anglican church," not fully understanding what an oxymoron that was. My Baptist ordination was "received" by the church (this was the "irregular" procedure Resurrection used to accept previously ordained clergy since the parish no longer had a bishop, and bishops perform all ordinations in the Anglican Communion). We shortly began to lead the prayer and communion ministry made up of lay people who help serve communion and pray for parishioners individually; Linda helped lead Alpha (an evangelism and newcomer formation program) and led prayers of the people.

We learned what it meant to vest—wearing albs or robes with a tabard of the seasonal color over them or for priests and deacons, a stole. We learned a whole new vocabulary including *Sanctus*, altar, preface, collect, and feast days like Maundy Thursday. Seasoned veterans in our Baptist church, we were now novices on a steep learning curve, but thoroughly enjoying the new insights.

In 1997, we became a part of a new church, Church of the Great Shepherd. At that time, I began working full time for a ministry, marketing a Lenten program for spiritual formation, but also served as a priest at Great Shepherd; Linda continued to work full time in speech and language therapy. She was also ordained to the diaconate at Great Shepherd ("irregularly") and began to function in that role. (Anglican deacons traditionally oversee care of the altar and ministry to those in need and read the Gospel.)

In July of 2001, Anglican Mission in the Americas (AMiA) was launched as a missionary outreach of the Anglican Church of Rwanda, whose archbishop expressed the desire to take orphaned evangelical Episcopal parishes under its wing, thereby making them a part of the worldwide Anglican Communion. The issue that threatened the unity of the Mission was the ordination of women to the priesthood; therefore, a moratorium on women's ordinations was put into place in AMiA in an effort to maintain unity.

Linda: This issue impacted us personally because the leadership of both churches we had been a part of was strongly opposed to women's ordination to the priesthood and we were very much in favor of it. We had a deep conviction that the scriptures supported an expanding role for women in the kingdom and in the Church. As I look back, I realize God was even then preparing me for a future ministry that, at the time, seemed highly unlikely.

Bill: In early 2003, Church of the Great Shepherd became a part of AMiA. That same year Great Shepherd outgrew the facility it was renting for worship and we, as leaders, began to talk about planting a new church. We departed for the new church plant with a public blessing from our new bishop, our pastor, and vestry. (The vestry is the governing board of an Anglican church.)

In the fall of 2004, our bishop *officially* ordained me to the priesthood and Linda to the diaconate. Receiving our ordination papers embossed with the seal of the Anglican Province of Rwanda brought home to us the significance of being a part of the worldwide Anglican Communion. In October of that year, Church of the Savior was officially planted in West Chicago as a parish committed to the three streams that had drawn us to Anglicanism in the first place: scripture, sacraments, and Spirit. We shared facilities with a local Reformed congregation.

This was an important and risky venture, and we were excited. God had brought us a long way—from a Billy Graham meeting in 1963 through our Baptist roots, first as laity and then for me as ordained clergy. He had walked with us through our brief journey into the Episcopal Church and then into the limbo status of two independent Anglican congregations. He nurtured us along the way through Bob Webber, his writings, and his friendship, and through new Anglican friends who encouraged us. And now, at 60, we were venturing out as possibly the oldest church planters ever.

Church of the Savior began with a deep commitment to allowing both women and men to use their gifts without limitations. Both men and women served on the vestry and preached, allowing Linda to be on the regular preaching rotation. At that time, the only door that was closed to women was ordination to the priesthood, because we continued to abide by the moratorium put in place by the Anglican Mission.

We feel especially privileged to share the liturgy with those who worship with us at Church of the Savior. The words we have repeated weekly for nearly twenty years carry us into the presence of God. We may come to church feeling discouraged or not inclined toward worship, but as we enter into the liturgy, we are carried and held by the words, by the community at Savior, by the worldwide Anglican Communion, and by the "angels and archangels and all the company of heaven."

In 2009, the Anglican Church in North America (ACNA) was formed as a parallel Anglican province in the U.S., with many different stripes of Anglicans coming under its umbrella, including the Anglican Mission in America. Perhaps the most surprising thing about ACNA was that churches on both sides of the women's ordination issue were willing to join together. Ordination to the priesthood was now open to women, both in AMiA and in ACNA, with some restrictions and accommodations.

Linda: In May of 2009, a tumor was incidentally discovered in the right atrium of my heart. Emergency open-heart surgery was done to remove the tumor and, as I recovered over the next few months, I realized very clearly that God had preserved my life. I began to ask the Lord, "What would you have me do with the rest of my life?"

God seemed to be saying that he wanted me to live into the call he had placed on my life back when Martha and I had prayed that our husbands would go to seminary. For the first time in my lifetime, the door was open for me to consider ordination to the priesthood. Step by step over the past year and a half, the door has opened wider, culminating in my passing the presbyter's (priest's) examination in December 2011. The way is clear for me to move forward with ordination in the very near future. Our parish is also now moving from the Anglican Mission into ACNA. (Linda has since been ordained as a priest.)

We have been on the Canterbury Trail for nearly twenty years . . . a journey we have shared as husband and wife, as a ministry team, and soon as co-pastors and priests. The journey has been rich, filled with joyful discoveries, disappointments, new horizons, and an increasing historical rootedness in the ancient Christian church.

In my study for the ordination examination, I learned the Latin phrase so significant to Anglicans: "*Lex orandi, lex credendi.*" We pray what we believe. We believe what we pray. Rather than having a confession as some faith traditions do, our beliefs are expressed in our prayers. The Anglican liturgy gives us words to pray what we believe and, as we pray, we believe it even more deeply. We hear our own voices echoing the voices from centuries past and centuries future . . .

Almighty God, to whom all hearts are open and all desires known . . .

Christ has died, Christ is risen, Christ will come again . . .

We join our voices with angels and archangels and all the company of heaven . . .

Go forth into the world in peace, rejoicing in the power of the Spirit. Alleluia! Alleluia!

PART
3

The Canterbury Trail
and Today's Churches

Paralleling
the Canterbury Trail

David Neff

> While my travels in the company of other worship renewal
> pilgrims may not end at Canterbury, the journey along the
> way has been transformative—ruinous, even, as Robert Web-
> ber promised. And I suspect that the trail and the tales
> will continue for many of us even beyond Canterbury.
>
> —Chris Alford, Graduate of the Robert E. Webber
> Institute for Worship Studies; Pastor of Epiclesis,
> a Non-Denominational Church Built on Webber's
> Ancient-Future Principles

In October 1982, I was confirmed in the Episcopal Church. After the ceremony, Gordon College English professor Thomas Howard walked up to me and said, "Welcome to this branch of the catholic church." Tom's writings had been an inspiration to me—from his 1967 spiritual classic, *Christ the Tiger,* to his 1981 handbook for worshipers, *The Liturgy Explained.* Two-and-a-half years after my confirmation, Tom left the Episcopal Church and was received into the Roman Catholic church.

In the early 1980s, I felt strongly drawn to the classic liturgy that connected our worship to the practices of early centuries. The way those ancient practices had been embodied in a liturgical spirituality at Saint Barnabas in Glen Ellyn, Illinois, gave it all a spiritual depth I had not experienced elsewhere. I was excited, and the Episcopal Church was obviously where I should choose to worship.

But for many drawn to old spiritualities and ancient liturgies, the charms of either Canterbury or Rome are not the only options and, to some (including this author), they have lost their sparkle and appeal as spiritual homes.

Many of us who were influenced by Bob Webber, or who were fellow travelers with him, made our pilgrimages to Canterbury. But Bob Webber never became an evangelist for the Episcopal Church or any other liturgical denomination. Why? Because he believed that evangelical congregations could be renewed through Ancient Future worship, catechesis, and spirituality.

The renewal of evangelical worship was the primary focus of his efforts. Bob may have belonged to Episcopal congregations like St. Barnabas and St. Mark's, but he spent his weekends pointing parched evangelicals to the waters of the ancient church, and he spent his weekdays teaching evangelical students about the wonders of worship properly understood.

I have come to understand that the allures of ecclesiastical Anglophilia can be a diversion from the really important thing: Canterbury is only one door to Ancient Future renewal.

Moving Forward to the Past

When Christians become dissatisfied with the state of the church, they often turn to the past, partly, perhaps, out of nostalgia, but also for perspective.

My Episcopal congregation recently had a good opportunity to gain perspective. As we celebrated our fiftieth anniversary, we planned special events such as "Party Like It's 1962" (our congregation's year of founding) and "Pray Like It's 1962." Praying like it's 1962 meant using the form of worship from the 1928 *Book of Common Prayer,* and hymns and service music from the Hymnal 1940.

Rather few members of our congregation were Episcopalians fifty years ago, so this was no exercise in nostalgia. Only a handful said the 1928 Prayer Book reminded them of their childhood. Far more people talked about the theological contrasts between the old form of the prayers and our new forms. (The newer forms are celebratory. The older forms are solemn and cautionary.)

A few weeks before my congregation's fiftieth anniversary service, I had another opportunity to gain perspective from an older form of worship. I attended a Holy Week service at a nearby Eastern Orthodox church. It was one of the "Bridegroom Matins." Orthodox worship was not entirely new to me. I have worshiped with an Orthodox church plant in a Baltimore schoolhouse, and I have worshiped with Ecumenical Patriarch Bartholomew in Istanbul. Nevertheless, this Holy Week service reminded me that Orthodox worship has a vocabulary of transcendence that has been muted in the Western church.

As Orthodox theologian Thomas Hopko recently told a Wheaton College audience, Christian worship, properly conceived, is a reflection of the worship that is going on in the heavenly temple. But it is more than a reflection. The church's earthly worship is an occasion for us to be lifted up and incorporated into heavenly realms and for the heavenly worship to break in to our consciousness.

Thus the Orthodox designed their liturgies and their worship spaces to emphasize this liturgical "wormhole" between heaven and earth. A worship vocabulary of transcendence can help us see spiritual realities beyond our normal perceptions. Every place can become a "thin place" if the worship space and action are so focused. Revisiting older worship forms can expand our worship vocabulary and allow those in congregational leadership—those who know the local believers best—to ring the changes on these themes as they relate to the spiritual needs of the worshipers and to the cultural messages they are receiving.

Ancient Future worship is not for antiquarians. That is why it is Ancient *Future* worship. It uses a rich and varied vocabulary from our Christian heritage to address the continually changing cultural currents that try to squeeze us into the world's mold. Those cultural moments tell us all sorts of stories about ourselves. They may say that we are individuals who are captains of our own destinies. (Think of the William Ernest Henley poem "Invictus" and the 2009 movie of the same name.) They may say that we cannot be fulfilled apart from a life of sexual variety. (Think of the distorted longings behind *Sex in the City*.) They may say that we can find meaning only when we are incessantly devoted to achieving career and workplace success. (Think of what drives the characters in *Mad Men*.)

The gospel, of course, tells us otherwise. And there are resources from the history of the church's worship that are useful in reshaping our perceptions of ourselves.

Past Imperfect

When evangelicals have sensed something wrong with church as they have known it, they often succumbed to the impulse to recover the same pure worship and practice experienced by the apostolic church. Scholars call this impulse "restoration-ism." Often (but not always) restorationism is anti-institutional and takes the form of house churches—not bad things in themselves, but often utopian, ahistorical, and short lived. Indeed, it was to impure and imperfect house churches that the Apostle Paul and, in the next generation, Clement of Rome wrote their letters of correction and exhortation. We have no reason to expect today's microcosms of restoration-ism to be different.

Sometimes restorationism takes the form of theological reductionism. This "no creed but Christ" tendency can be seen at work in the Church of Christ, some Baptist groups, and the radical Reformation. The gospel is indeed simple, but after the apostolic age, the church took centuries to work out the questions it faced. Most of those questions stemmed from its uncertain relationship with Judaism. Creeds and wor-ship practices ended up affirming the basics of the revelation to Israel, but with deeper understandings gained through reflection on the implications of Jesus' life, death, and res-urrection. Trying to jump back over the church's wrestling with key questions about the Christ and his relationship to the one God of Israel is asking for trouble.

As that post-apostolic church struggled with tensions over its relation to Judaism and to the revelation in the Hebrew scriptures, it ended up affirming those scriptures. But along the way it also said hurtful things to and about Jews. Similarly, as it struggled with questions about the body and sexuality, it ended up with a qualified affirmation of the goodness of the physical world. (At least the results were better than the anti-body alternatives taught by Gnostics and, later, Albigenses.) There were also questions about the role of law in the Christian life and questions about the relation of the church to the state.

According to my lights, none of these questions were settled completely and satisfactorily. However, we can, at the very least, recognize that the answers the church achieved created categories and boundaries for future discussions.

To start from scratch is an invitation to walk down the same blind alleys we have visited before.

Indeed, the restorationist impulse sometimes ends up in downright heresy—as it did with Mormonism in the 19th century and Armstrongism in the 20th.

A Return to the Sources

How can we turn to the past for perspective without succumbing either to the problems of restorationism or to nostalgic romanticism, another oft-exercised option? We can do so by focusing on a third "r." In addition to restorationism and romanticism, there is *ressourcement*.

Robert Webber's notion of an Ancient Future church parallels those of a group of mid-twentieth-century French Roman Catholic theologians who, in the years before the second Vatican Council in the 1960s, regrounded Catholic theology in the apostolic and post-apostolic sources. They brought renewal to many corners of Catholic theology, worship, and practical living by helping the faithful to encounter afresh the scriptures and early Christian writers and by calling their attention to how these could speak to twentieth-century challenges. Broadly speaking, the church had become stuck, using as its reference points the theologians of the Middle Ages and the retrenchment in response to the work of the Protestant Reformers. But these twentieth-century theologians advocated a return to the sources. Their rallying cry was *ad fontes* (i.e., turn to the fonts of ancient thought and practice). And their name for what they were doing was *ressourcement*. They hoped to approach the challenges of contemporary society afresh—but not without a deep understanding of the early history.

The work of these twentieth-century theologians provided a new framework for the second Vatican Council. Although Catholic liberals and conservatives debate what was actually accomplished at Vatican II, the Council was nevertheless able to grapple with important issues such as the encounter with non-Christian religions, the nature of the church, the role of the laity, the importance of scripture, religious liberty, and the reformation of the liturgy. It was an important time of self-criticism and openness to change.

Bob Webber was hoping for something similar as he encouraged fellow evangelicals to encounter the classical creeds, the writings of the early church, and historic approaches to spirituality. He looked for self-evaluation and openness to change rooted in the Christian sources.

If you read the autobiographical sections of Bob's books, you will find that before he began looking to the ancient sources, he experienced a religion with no mystery, no sense of Christ's triumph, and no use for beauty. His religion was on the defensive. It offered neat, rational answers to messy questions that were too big for such explanations. He had placed his faith in a religion of rules rather than in a living participation in Christ. He saw a religion focused narrowly on the cross rather than a biblical faith that proclaimed the full sweep of God's intention for his creation.

He also saw a society in transition. He saw the demise of the rationalistic modernism that had called forth the equally rationalistic fundamentalism in which he had been raised. He saw the rise of postmodern society in which mystery, experience, beauty, nonverbal communication, and premodern mindsets all had a place.

This postmodern society, which loudly rejected controlling metanarratives, badly needed a bold articulation of the big biblical story. Bob reached back to the second-century theologian Irenaeus of Lyons for that bold proclamation. Irenaeus built on the Apostle Paul's notion of Christ as the Second or Last Adam to argue that in his humanity he had righted everything that the First Adam had managed to mess up. Thus, Christ had become the head of the new humanity that would inhabit a renewed creation.

Irenaeus was arguing against a group of heretics that despised the material world and taught that the Christ did not take on a truly human body. By articulating this narrative of "recapitulation," as it was called, Irenaeus showed that Christ's incarnation in human flesh and his redemption of the entire created material order were essential to Christian faith.

If you go looking for this theology of recapitulation in evangelical theology books, you will find very little. Stan Grenz was one of the rare evangelical theologians who made use of

Irenaeus's scheme. Like Bob Webber, Grenz saw the importance of this way of framing the biblical story for postmodern ears. Unfortunately, most evangelical theologians have ignored this theme and its narrative persuasiveness.

Just because postmoderns in the West have declared a moratorium on grand metanarratives doesn't mean that we have a shortage of stories competing to define us as human beings. Worshipers need to be aware of all the lesser narratives that influence us on a daily basis. By defining the problem we face and naming a solution, these stories define us.

The consumer narrative is, perhaps, most prevalent. Problem: You are unhappy because you lack the right consumer goods, wear the wrong clothes, or use the wrong toiletries. Solution: Buy and use the product advertised. What is the human person in this narrative? Someone who seeks after things, acquires them, and finds meaning in them.

There is a parallel careerist narrative. In it, the problem is lack of achievement. The solution is either a tool for getting ahead (perhaps the right smartphone or tablet computer) or a status symbol that signifies achievement (a luxury car, perhaps, or the platinum version of a particular credit card). The good life is described by an arc of advancement in wealth and power.

There is also an entertainment narrative—a variation on the consumer narrative. Thanks to technical and cultural innovations that date back to the seventies, we now live in a niche entertainment culture calibrated to reinforce our individualism. That culture audaciously tells us that our lives are measured by the distracting amusements we consume rather than by the creative work or loving service we perform. Amazingly, entertainment industry celebrities (think Oprah) can now carry more weight with public opinion than leaders of government, academe, or industry. Indeed, even the business leaders who fascinate us most are enmeshed in the way we entertain ourselves—Steve Jobs and Mark Zuckerberg, for example.

But the gospel tells us something different about ourselves. Our story is not just about today or tomorrow or our own lifespans. Our story stretches back to the beginning of time and forward to a final consummation. At the center of the story is the ideal human being, the Second Adam, who is the head of a new humanity. Our lives are both bigger and smaller than the competing narratives would suggest. They are bigger because our decisions and our actions are part and parcel of the destiny of the entire cosmos. They are smaller because they are overshadowed and relativized by the one perfect life.

The Church Search

When we find ourselves reoriented to this biblical story, where are we to find spiritual and social sustenance? Where are we to worship and fellowship?

Clergy and worship leaders have the option of leading their people back to the sources. But lay people are likely to have to choose some existing framework. This is what I did as a former pastor and religion teacher when I wanted to let myself be shaped by the ancient forms of worship. I walked the Canterbury Trail. I joined the Episcopal Church.

I could, of course, have found solid liturgy, Eucharistic worship, and a historically and biblically informed faith in other places: Lutheran, Catholic, Orthodox.

Today, too, there is a parallel fellowship of North American Anglican congregations outside the Episcopal Church. There is also an independent network of about fifty pastors and worship leaders that is trying to implement the principles of the Call to an Ancient Evangelical Future in a variety of denominational settings—Baptist, Methodist, Presbyterian, Anglican, and one group in "pre-denominational" mode. As I write, that Ancient Future Faith Network is planning its first face-to-face meeting. May this new network flourish.

There should be no monopoly on contemporary worship informed by ancient sources. The Ancient Future perspective, with one eye on our changing context and one eye on the ancient sources, is essential for the constant renewal of worship and church life. It is my prayer that many congregations find renewal in this Ancient Future mode.

The Multiple Paths
on the Canterbury Trail

Thomas Buchan

To believe that the Holy Spirit has grounded and empowered the church's tradition is to affirm and trust
the Spirit's continuing guidance as the church has
sought to understand and embody the gospel ever more
fully in its communal life and mission to the world.
Ancient Christian interpretation and reflection were
especially astute and gifted in the ability to hear
and sing the music of the gospel.

—*Christopher Hall, Chancellor, Eastern University,*
St. Davids, Pennsylvania, and Dean, Palmer Theological
Seminary, St. Davids, Pennsylvania

I n the title *Evangelicals on the Canterbury Trail*, Robert
Webber deployed the accessible and attractive metaphor of the spiritual life as journey. Like many useful and
powerful images, the metaphor in Webber's title worked—
and continues to work—precisely because it was not rigidly
propositional. As a symbol, *Evangelicals on the Canterbury Trail*
could lend itself to interpretation in numerous ways. It could
identify those, like Webber, who had disaffiliated from prior
ecclesial communities to be received into and confirmed

in the Episcopal Church. It could, however, also be used to name the experiences of feeling attracted to and appreciative of traditional liturgical patterns of worship, but without any intention of becoming Episcopalian or Anglican. Additionally, it could provide a non-threatening image for answering the questions, on the one hand, of those who did *not* feel the attraction of the Anglican liturgical tradition (especially parents of previously nonliturgically inclined Wheaton College students!), and, on the other, of "non-evangelical" Episcopalians curious about the evangelical "pilgrims" in their midst.

In this metaphor of the "Canterbury Trail," Webber's brilliant and ingenious gift of saying—and not saying—so many things at once is on display. Webber's name for the journey he himself took is warm, folksy, and perhaps even mildly quaint. It is an appealing image that conveys an invitation to share, at the very least, in the *story* of another's personal voyage of spiritual discovery even if one is not inclined to become a pilgrim oneself. Webber knew that not everyone would want to make the journey he had made. He did not ask them to. Nor did he ask for agreement or endorsement, but merely encouraged understanding and empathy. On the other hand, it is clear that Webber wished to encourage and welcome those who might be interested in walking the trail with him, whether or not they would eventually "arrive" at his own Anglican destination. Furthermore, though the original edition's personal narratives all told the stories of men and women who had become Episcopalians, Webber understood himself to be describing a phenomenon that was also taking place in "Presbyterian, Lutheran, Methodist, and other historic [mainline] denominations as well."

In Webber's book, therefore, the Canterbury Trail could be used as a way to name a wide range of approaches to historic Christianity, liturgical worship, or the Anglican tradition from a variety of starting points (Baptist, Presbyterian, Pentecostal, non-denominational, etc.) and without a programmatic or prescriptive outcome. Webber believed that walking the Canterbury Trail could be beneficial even for those who would not become Episcopalian as he had. On the other hand, however, at its most focused, the Canterbury Trail was quite obviously an image for becoming Episcopalian. This was the story told seven times in the book's original version through Webber's own experience and the experience of each of the book's other pilgrims. Though he was clear that no one was under any obligation to make the same journey he had, Webber was no less clear in his identification of historic Christianity, liturgical worship, and Anglicanism with the Episcopal Church. For Webber himself, "Canterbury" was the Episcopal Church; the Episcopal Church was historic, liturgical, and Anglican Christianity; and to be Episcopalian was to be a Christian in the historic, liturgical, and Anglican tradition. Interestingly, however, even in 1985, it was not the case that being Episcopalian was the only way to identify as an Anglican Christian in the United States.

■ ■ ■

Over the last decade or so, the new diversity of Anglicanism in North America has received a great deal of attention, and for good reasons. In all of this, however, what has frequently gone unnoticed or unspoken is the extent to which there have existed Anglican alternatives to the Episcopal Church for a period of time in excess of 100 years. The Reformed Episcopal Church—itself now a founding member of 2009's Anglican Church in North America—began in 1873, at least in part from concerns (as its online historical review states) "over the excessive ritualism and exclusive attitude of the Protestant Episcopal Church toward other denominations."[1] Reformed Episcopal Church sources portray one of the major underlying concerns of the denomination's founding as "a concern . . . to protect what can be called the Anglicanism of the English Reformation" against an American Anglo-Catholic reappraisal of the value of pre-Reformation traditions. The Reformed Episcopal Church regards itself as "another denomination (though not another church)." Its Declaration of Principles is "not an attempt to depart from historic Anglican beliefs. Rather, they are an expression of a return to the old paths of the Protestant Episcopal Church and our English Reformers."

The same kind of impulse to theologically and ecclesiastically clarify and define Anglicanism—often in opposition to other expressions—has been at least part of what has informed the emergence of several other North American Anglican alternatives to the Episcopal Church during the course of the latter half of the twentieth century. The Orthodox Anglican Church (1964) and the similarly named but ecclesiastically distinct Anglican Orthodox Church (founded in 2001 with reference to developments in the early 1960s) both trace their origins back to the early 1960s. The American Episcopal Church followed in 1968. In 1972, the Anglican

---

1. *http://rechurch.org/recus/?MIval=/recweb/foundations.html&display=overview.*

Church of North America was founded, followed in 1977 by the Anglican Catholic church and the Anglican Province of Christ the King. The United Episcopal Church of North America was formed in 1981. By 1991, splits within the American Episcopal Church (1968) and the Anglican Catholic church (1977) led to the formation of two new denominations: the Anglican Church in America (1991) and the Anglican Province of America (which dates its founding back to the formation of the American Episcopal Church in 1968). The International Communion of the Charismatic Episcopal Church (1992), the Episcopal Missionary Church (1992), and the Anglican Episcopal Church, Celtic Rite (1993) all emerged in the first half of the last decade of the twentieth century.

Closer to our own cultural moment, the continuing formation of Anglican alternatives to the Episcopal Church—in particular the Anglican Mission in the Americas (AMiA, founded 2000, originally the "Anglican Mission in America," then revised to the "Anglican Mission in the Americas") and the Anglican Church in North America (ACNA, founded 2009)—have generated much attention and interest, not only among their adherents and Episcopalians, but also among journalists, scholars, and curious Christians, especially evangelicals, from other denominations. What is occasionally less well known is that since 2000, in addition to AMiA and ACNA, five other Anglican modes have also emerged in North America: the Anglican Episcopal Church (2000), the Christian Episcopal Church (ca. 2002), the Convocation of Anglicans in North America (2006), the Anglican Episcopal Church International (2008), and the establishment under

Pope Benedict XVI's *Anglicanorum Coetibus* of Anglican Use personal ordinariates (2009).

When these developments are taken into account, it becomes almost impossible not to notice that there are—and have been for some time—more ways than one of "being Anglican" in North America. Indeed, in the tensions generated by theological and ecclesiastical disputes among the varieties of North American Anglicans, one is now often asked to clarify whether one is "Episcopalian" or "Anglican." If "Anglican," one may well be asked to stipulate what kind of Anglican one professes to be. This way of parsing ecclesiastical identity would not have been totally unheard of in earlier decades—to some extent this is the blessing and the burden of the *via media*, the "middle way" so central to Anglican theology, liturgy, and history. To be candid, contests over who or what is authentically Anglican have always been a part of being Anglican. Recently, however, the number of venues *in* which and the degree *to* which the dividing line has come to be articulated as one that passes *between* "being Episcopalian" and "being Anglican" has grown far more prevalent. (As an Episcopal priest formerly teaching in an evangelical seminary, I have been asked more than a few times over the last several years, "Are you Episcopalian or Anglican?" I have found that most of my interrogators have been less than fully satisfied with my simple, comprehensive, and true answer: "Yes.")

■ ■ ■

What can be said of these, by almost all accounts, unhappy divisions? Webber's Canterbury Trail was a welcoming avenue to a "Return to Mystery," a deeper "Experience of Worship," an encounter with "Sacramental Reality," a means for finding "Spiritual Identity," a way of "Embracing the Whole Church," and a "Holistic Spirituality." I am convinced that these six aspects of what Anglicanism has to offer have remained constant. It is no wonder to me that women and men continue to feel drawn to the Anglican liturgical and spiritual tradition that drew Webber, his original six pilgrims, me, and so many others.

At times, however, I do wonder whether too much has changed for Webber's image of *Evangelicals on the Canterbury Trail*—so right for its time—to do now what it did then. Are we pressing his device past its limits? Is it time for us to leave the Canterbury Trail? Have we passed so many forks that speaking of multiple paths on the same trail has become difficult to imagine or untenable? Do we need a new metaphor to name the experiences of Anglicans in North America?

I do not pretend to have definitive answers to these questions. They are, for me, not merely theoretical, but intensely and intimately practical. Over the course of the last twenty years, I have endured the pain of parting company with fellow pilgrims more often than I care to recall. For those of my beloved friends who have taken "other paths," and for those of us who have remained Webber's "main-line," there have been moments of unspeakable grief arising from our separations from one another despite our mutual affections, despite our common identity in one Lord, one faith, one baptism.

Are we all still on the Canterbury Trail? It is hard to tell sometimes. Some of us are in full communion with

Canterbury, but in impaired communion with other dioceses or provinces of the Anglican Communion. Others of us are in full communion with dioceses or provinces that are themselves in communion with Canterbury, but are not in full or unimpaired communion with the Episcopal Church. Of late, there is word from other places of the status of relationships of communion seeming to change from moment to moment. It can be hard in these days to know for sure exactly where one is going. How much more difficult is it to know where others are headed?

And yet, for all of this, from time to time as one walks on, over the hills and through the trees comes the refrain of the pilgrim song—distant, hard to hear without listening carefully, but there nonetheless. On occasion, one reaches a crossroads, and finds a sister, a brother, long unseen, feared lost, but here and ready to share a meal that is ours by Another's invitation and command. We walk on parted ways, but not without faith in the One who has called us, not without hope that we, though separated, are one in Him, and not without love which "bears all things, believes all things, hopes all things, endures all things." And so, with thanks to Robert Webber and apologies to St. Paul, may faith, hope, and love journey on.

CHAPTER

14

Robert Webber: The Man of the Future and the Church of the Future

Reggie Kidd

I was ordained an Anglican priest in 2004. The journey to that day began in 1987 when I noticed an advertisement for *Evangelicals on the Canterbury Trail*. I bought the book, read it in one sitting, and, consequently, Robert Webber helped set the course for my future life and ministry.

—*The Rev. Peter Matthews, St. Patrick's Anglican Church, Lexington, Kentucky*

Recently, I was explaining to a friend how Bob Webber had transformed my worship sensibility by introducing me to worship practices of the church's first half-millennium. My friend offered a knowing nod and a roll of the eyes: "I get it. The pendulum swings. A lot of people are in reaction to what seems to pass for worship these days, so I can see why going back to liturgy and mystery is the current fad."

Fads fade. Markets devour their children. For years, I followed Bob Webber's writings from afar, observing how even he labored to stay ahead of the fad- and market-curve.

His language morphed from "blended" to "convergent" to "ancient future" worship. I remember, after we became friends, his disappointment that his book *Journey to Jesus*—an updating of the ancient church's method of baptismal preparation—failed to get much traction.

What endures? What bears promise for the future?

With apologies to my eye-rolling friend, I believe Bob Webber was on to something eternal, indeed transcendent. With his personal charisma, Bob had all the characteristics of a modern-day Pied Piper. He had a mischievous smile, a rapier sharp wit, hair-on-fire energy, and an unparalleled ability to crystallize massive ideas in memorable quips. He could have built a following all about himself. But he was after a following for Someone else.

What gives Bob Webber's legacy "legs" is that he caught a glimmer of the same "hand from a hidden country" that C. S. Lewis described when he wrote of the way Holy Communion affected him: "Here a hand from a hidden country touches not only my soul but my body. . . . Here is big medicine and strong magic."[2] Bob saw the whole of worship as an assent to the touch of that hand. Worship of the Father, through the Son, and in the Holy Spirit is where big medicine heals and strong magic transforms.

Bob sensed that the enchantment of the African landscape of his childhood bore witness to truths that the science-idolizing West can ignore for only so long. Incarnation had forever made heaven and earth mutually permeable. He

---

2. C.S. Lewis, *Letters to Malcolm, Chiefly on Prayer* (New York: Harcourt, 1964), 103.

perceived that the fundamentalism of his upbringing was both right and wrong about the Bible—right in its unyielding loyalty to scripture, wrong in its prideful sectarianism. He had a gut instinct that the "liturgical renewal" movement, which began with French monks discovering plainsong chant in the early nineteenth century, was a harbinger of change in worship for everybody, liturgically inclined or not. Bob had a hunch, therefore, that the next generation of worship leaders would need historical and theological, as well as musical chops.

Bob's greatest gift to us is that he challenged, invited, cajoled, and teased us into reacquainting ourselves with the biblical Christ, with the aid of the first generations of biblical interpreters and worship-practitioners. Bob loved to quote Melito of Sardis's Easter sermon of A.D. 195, a breathtaking portrait of who our Savior is and of what he came to do for us:

> "I am he who destroys death,
> and triumphs over the enemy,
> and crushes Hades,
> and binds the strong man,
> and bears humanity off to the heavenly heights.
> It is I," says the Christ.[3]

And Bob was fond of invoking the Eucharistic Thanksgiving attributed to Hippolytus (ca. A.D. 215):

> In fulfillment of your will, he stretched out his hands
> in suffering
> to free from suffering those who place their trust in you.

---

3. Melito of Sardis, "Peri Pascha" (On the Passover), *http://www.kerux. com/documents/KeruxV4N1A1.asp*

He freely accepted the death to which he was
　　handed over,

in order to destroy death and to shatter the chains
　　of the evil one,

to trample underfoot the powers of hell and to lead
　　the righteous into life,

to fix the boundaries of death and to manifest the
　　resurrection.[4]

Bob believed that the ancient church's worship emphasized dimensions of Christ's person and work that were the
antidote to the malaise of contemporary worship. He understood that evangelicals—weary of trying to make the penal
substitutionary aspect of the atonement fix everything—were
ready to be reminded of other dimensions of our victorious
Christ's work. Not only has Christ's death taken away the
guilt of our sin, but, as the ancients taught us, it has begun
the making new of all things.

Moreover, he had an inkling that evangelicals—no longer content to do their theology merely in their heads—were
ready for a bracing voice from the early days of Christian the-
ologizing, when theology was embodied and indeed forged
in prayer, in song, in sacrament, in service.

As Bob once blogged:

The emphasis of biblical and ancient God-directed worship
is ultimately about the victory of God over all the powers of
evil. In worship, we remember God's saving acts in history,
and we anticipate the consummation of God's rescue at

---

4. Hippolytus, Eucharistic liturgy in *Apostolic Tradition*.

the end of history. This theme is sung, proclaimed, and enacted in all the liturgies of the early church.[5]

To me, one of the happy features of the 1979 revision of the *Book of Common Prayer* is the echoing of the ancient church's language in Eucharistic Prayer A: "He stretched out his arms upon the cross, and offered himself in obedience to your will, a perfect sacrifice for the whole world."

Every time I hear those words, I cannot but think also of Athanasius, the fourth-century bishop of Alexandria. In Jesus' "outstretched arms," Athanasius saw our Redeemer's loving intention to bring into unity those who are separated:

> Here again, we see the fitness of his death and of those outstretched arms: it was that He might draw his ancient people with the one and the Gentiles with the other, and join both together in Himself.[6]

On the cross, Jesus joined God's world and ours, and at the same time brought together people long hostile to one another. That cruciform pattern sums up Bob Webber's own life: drawing one group of people with one hand and an adversarial group with the other, then joining them together in worship in Christ. Herein lies what I think will prove to be most enduring and, like Lewis's "hidden hand," transcendent about his vision for worship.

The faith Jesus embodied in his life, established by his death and resurrection, and now nurtures in his ascension

---

5. Robert Webber, *Ancient Future Worship* newsletter (February 2004, *http://www.ancientfutureworship.com/newsletter/200402.html*).

6. Athanasius of Alexandria, *The Incarnation of the Word of God* (25:5). Compare to Ephesians 2:11–22.

is a subtle intertwining of what Charles Williams might have called "coinherences." Bob had the profoundest sense of how these coinherences work: Mystery (God's ultimate incomprehensibility) needs Incarnation (in Jesus, God has shown us his face), and vice versa. Scripture (verbal communication) needs Sacrament (symbolic communication), and vice versa. Doxology (it's all about God's glory) needs Conversion (God gave his Son to glorify me), and vice versa. Catholicity (there is but one universal church) needs Orthodoxy (that same church is called to doctrinal fidelity and holiness of life), and vice versa. Community (the centripetal energy of the gospel) needs Mission (the centrifugal energy of the gospel), and vice versa.

The reality is that we are not all called to the same tasks, nor uniformly wired with the same instincts, nor uniformly attuned to the same resonances. Bob understood that the Spirit builds the Body of Christ for interdependence. The original publication of this little volume concluded by calling us to realize our need for each other. As a self-designated "evangelical," Bob acknowledged that he was stepping into a liturgical world that had been alien to him as a youth, but from which he had come to learn mystery, worship, sacraments, historical identity, ecumenical affirmation, and holistic spirituality. In the last chapter of that original volume, he asked liturgical Christians—not always necessarily burdened with evangelical sensibilities—to consider how "born again" types like Webber himself might enrich their worship: personal faith, doctrinal orthodoxy, Bible centeredness, and missional sensibility. One kind of worship without the other, he maintained in that first edition, "is a truncated

Christianity. We need both. Consequently, evangelicals and the liturgical tradition need each other. . . . (W)e must rise above . . . pettiness, above spiritual pride, and affirm the whole church of Christ and our need for each other."[7]

What makes Bob Webber a man for the future—with a word for the future of the church? He points us to Christ on the cross, where heaven and earth are bridged, and where all things will one day find their reconciliation:

> Lord Jesus Christ, you stretched out your arms of love on the hard wood of the cross that everyone might come within the reach of your saving embrace: So clothe us in your Spirit that we, reaching forth our hands in love, may bring those who do not know you to the knowledge and love of you; for the honor of your Name. Amen.[8]

---

7. Webber, *Evangelicals on the Canterbury Trail* (Harrisburg, PA: Morehouse, 1985), 171.

8. *Book of Common Prayer* (New York: Church Publishing, 1979), 101.

AFTERWORD

Barry Taylor

When I was approached to contribute to this revision of Robert Webber's seminal book, I was both honored and a little bit uncertain. I knew Bob, but not that well. I was introduced to him by a friend; we were at a few conferences together and shared a couple of seminars once or twice. He was a lovely man in so many ways—generous, thoughtful, deeply reflective, and at times quite fervent and decidedly convinced of his views. We were at different ends of a theological spectrum on many things, but that never got in the way of friendship, and we shared a common feeling that all things related to Christian faith and spirituality needed to shift. We had lots of post-conference conversations about this or that.

Where we differed was in terms of directions to follow. My basic orientation is that the way forward is forward; we have, of course, rich tradition and history to help and inform, but recovering historical practices will never be enough in my mind. For Bob, however, that seemed to be a dominant thread. We nudged each other about interpretations of all things postmodern and their negative or positive possibilities for the church.

And, even though I outwardly at least fit all the criteria that Bob outlines in the book for why evangelicals might find their way into Anglicanism, I would call my own story "An Accidental Anglican" because that's how it seems to me. I didn't plan it; it sort of just happened. Was it destiny, fate, or happy accident? I don't know. I guess it all depends on how one views the activity and interaction of the Divine in our lives. All I can say is that I am happy to be here.

■ ■ ■

Bob's turn to Anglicanism came at a particular point in the history of the church—the beginning of the end of modernity some say—and the collapsing of so many unnecessary boundaries that accompanied it. Bob's evangelical world was decidedly separate from mainline denominations; in fact mainline churches were like forbidden fruit. He was part of a large number of people who exchanged a particular expression of their faith for a more ritualized, sacramental version during the latter part of the twentieth century. In today's world, those lines are much less firmly drawn; for me, personally, they always were.

It seems to me the rise of liturgical interest among evangelicals has taken two distinct forms. For Bob and others, it usually meant a formalizing of a relationship, a movement out of one world into another. Bob's story in this book describes his own trepidation at how his shift to membership in the Episcopal Church would be received by his evangelical peers. It was a time when denominational and theological boundaries were still held more firmly and it was a big thing to walk across those divides. Defensiveness and territorialism were still rife; not that they don't still exist, but times have changed.

The second dynamic, the one that has emerged in the past ten or fifteen years, has been different. It hasn't necessarily involved the exchanging of denominational affiliations, and is just as likely to involve the appropriation of certain practices within the horizons of evangelicalism itself. It is not as unusual today to find evangelical communities celebrating Lent, going on pilgrimages, holding Taizé worship services, or using liturgies and lectionaries to shape their worship. Fuller Seminary, where I teach, has a Roman Catholic group and an Episcopal group that meet and worship together, as well as many other diverse groups—something that would have been considered anathema not that long ago. There is reciprocity. Evangelical and Charismatic and non-denominational groups, which tend to be more open to the shifting of cultural nuances and needs, offered their charisms to Anglicans and other mainline churches seeking to resonate with their environments. Things like Fresh Expressions and Alternative Worship have emerged in more traditional environments, not only in the United Kingdom but here in the United States.

Like a great many theologians and commentators on all things religious, I believe there are seismic shifts happening in the world of religion and belief that will impact every "trail." It seems to me what Bob identified in his thinking those many years ago was a fissure, a crack in a wall that continues to expand to this day.

■ ■ ■

In his Introduction to this book, Bob identified six things that for him were the reasons he joined the Anglican community. As I read and reflect on them, I can understand how and why they captured him, particularly given the state of the Christian world back then. A sense of mystery in religious experience, a Christ-centered worship experience, a sacramental reality, a historical identity, a feeling of being part of Christ's entire church, and a holistic spirituality are a compelling set of gifts that Bob found and grew to cherish in Anglicanism.

I wonder if the lines are quite so clearly demarcated these days. The trails converge a little more now, and many of the things he named—like wanting to feel connected to the wider church, desiring a more holistic spirituality, seeking a more Christ-centered worship experience, or even hungering for a more sacramental view of life and faith—are much more engaged by a wider portion of the church, regardless of liturgical rootedness or not. Indeed, much of Bob's own work went toward casting those seeds as far and wide as he could fling them. In those days when evangelical Christianity was marked by an almost belligerent commitment to certainty (not to say that has entirely gone away), it is easy to see why someone would want to be in an environment where mystery, doubt, wonder, and beauty are acknowledged and celebrated. I love the Anglican sense of mystery as well, but to be honest, I find it in many places today where it was once unwelcome. The hunger for a more open and inquiring faith, rather than abstract believing, has drawn mystery out into the light a bit more.

■ ■ ■

I am not sure any of Bob's reasons for embarking on the Canterbury Trail are necessarily mine. Those things he named are equally as important to me, but I don't think any of them are the specific or necessarily identifiable reasons for which

I find myself in the Anglican church today. In fact, if I were to give a specific reason for my own engagement, I would say "space." I have realized over the years that space is important to me.

One of the main struggles I have encountered throughout my life's journey has been with finding space, finding room—the room to breathe freely, the room to think, to grapple with issues and ideas, and particularly within the church to think theologically. This remains the great gift of the Anglican church to me. It seems, to me, to be one of the unique and perhaps most underrated gifts of the Canterbury Trail. I talked about that with Bob once. We noted the freedom that a more open theological horizon afforded both of us, and the challenge it could be to find ourselves in more closed environments where group thinking held more of a sway.

In these often polarized times in which we find ourselves, space for different views, theological positions, or ecclesiological perspectives is a rare commodity. Sadly, it seems, that space is somewhat besieged at present in the wider church; the beauty of Anglicanism seems to be imploding under the strain of various and oppositional responses to the cultural shifts of the digital age. But I have found room to breathe, to continue my own theological journey, and to "think out loud."

Whether the metaphor is one of "trail" or "space," Bob's original testimony in this book, as well as the new testimonies of those who have joined his journey, witness that such a thing still exists by surprising—even accidental in my case— grace. Thanks be to God.

ABOUT THE CONTRIBUTORS

THOMAS BUCHAN is a priest of the Episcopal Church and the associate professor of church history at Nashotah House Theological Seminary. He earned degrees in Biblical and Theological Studies (including coursework in church history with Robert Webber) at Wheaton College. He later earned his doctorate in theological and religious studies at Drew University, where he was a graduate research assistant on several volumes of *The Ancient Christian Commentary on Scripture*, edited by Thomas Oden. From 2006–2012, Thomas was the associate professor of Christian theology on Asbury Theological Seminary's Florida Dunnam Campus in Orlando, Florida. He and his wife, Shelly, have two children.

JON HALL is the rector of St. Martin's Episcopal Church in Ellisville, Missouri. He graduated from Centenary College of Louisiana in 1986 and received a master's in counseling from Asbury Theological Seminary in Wilmore, Kentucky, in 2003. He completed the course for a Diploma in Anglican Studies from General Theological Seminary in New York City in 2005. He was ordained in the Diocese of Lexington the same year and served St. Philip's Episcopal Church in Harrodsburg, Kentucky, from 2005 to 2010. He and his wife, Colleen, enjoy living in the St. Louis area with their daughter, Abbey.

REGGIE KIDD has taught at Reformed Theological Seminary in Orlando, Florida, since 1990, where he is a professor of New Testament. In 2001, Reggie also began teaching at the Robert E. Webber Institute for Worship Studies, where, thanks to Bob's friendship and contagious enthusiasm, he began to think of himself as a student of "the way of the liturgy." Since 2008, Reggie and his family have been participating in the life of the Cathedral Church of St. Luke, Orlando. He holds two master's degrees from Westminster Theological Seminary in Glenside, Pennsylvania, and a Ph.D. in Christian origins from Duke University in Durham, North Carolina. His writings include *With One Voice: Discovering Christ's Song in Our Worship* (Baker Books, 2005). Since Bob's death, Reggie has contributed a regular column on the ancient-future perspective for *Worship Leader Magazine.*

DAVID MADEIRA is the associate director of music at St. Bartholomew's Episcopal Church in Nashville, Tennessee. He teaches music theory at Belmont University and is a composer, hymn writer, and choral conductor. He is currently a doctoral student at the Robert E. Webber Institute for Worship Studies and resides in Franklin, Tennessee, with his wife, Elizabeth, and son, Nathaniel.

ANNA MASI is an officially sponsored Lay Ministry seminarian on behalf of St. Peter's Anglican Church in Tallahassee, Florida, and the Gulf-Atlantic Diocese of Anglican Church in North America. She will graduate from Duke Divinity School in May 2013 with her Master of Divinity, after which she intends to pursue her Ph.D. and enter non-profit work. Her current studies focus on the intersection of sacraments and disabilities. *Note*: Her friend Matt is now Brother Matt, O.S.B. and intends to take his solemn vows in July 2013 at St. Vincent Archabbey in Latrobe, Pennsylvania. He and Anna are still close, and Anna visits him at St. Vincent's regularly.

DAVID NEFF is editor in chief and vice president of *Christianity Today.* As organist/choirmaster of St. Barnabas Episcopal Church in Glen Ellyn, Illinois, he composes and arranges music for the choir. He serves on the boards of the Robert E. Webber Institute for Worship Studies, Orange Park, Florida, and the Robert E. Webber Center at Trinity School for Ministry in Ambridge, Pennsylvania. He is vice chair of the board of the National Association of Evangelicals.

BILL RICHARDSON is the rector of Church of the Savior in Wheaton, Illinois, an Anglican church affiliated with the Anglican

Church in North America. He graduated from California State University at Long Beach and received a Master of Divinity from Talbot Theological Seminary in La Mirada, California. He lives in Wheaton with his wife.

LINDA RICHARDSON is a priest and serves as associate pastor at Church of the Savior in Wheaton, Illinois. She graduated from California State University at Long Beach and received a master's degree in speech pathology from the same institution. She also earned a certificate in spiritual direction from Christos Center for Spiritual Formation in Minneapolis.

LESTER RUTH teaches worship history at the Robert E. Webber Institute for Worship Studies, Orange Park, Florida, which is where he got to know Robert Webber. He also is research professor of Christian worship at Duke Divinity School. He taught at Asbury Theological Seminary and Yale Divinity School after receiving his Ph.D. in liturgical history at the University of Notre Dame. A native of Texas, he served as a United Methodist minister for several years before becoming a professor. Never an Anglican himself, Lester delights nonetheless that some of his favorite early Methodists, including Charles and John Wesley, were Anglican priests.

BARRY TAYLOR is an Episcopal priest serving at All Saints' Beverly Hills, where he is senior associate rector. He is co-director for the Creative and Emerging Ministry project of the Diocese of Los Angeles. Barry is also artist-in-residence and affiliate professor for theology and culture for the Brehm Center for Theology Worship and the Arts at Fuller Theological Seminary in Pasadena, as well as moonlighting as an instructor in the School of Advertising at Pasadena's Art Center College of Design. He travels globally addressing issues of church and culture, has written a number of books on faith and culture, and writes and makes music with friends. He also drinks PG Tips tea in profuse amounts, because that's what you do when you are a Brit in Los Angeles.

ROBERT WEBBER earned his Th.D. in historical theology at Concordia Theological Seminary in St. Louis. Beginning in 1968 and continuing for many years, he served as Professor of Theology at Wheaton College. Early in his career he began exploring and promoting the value of the early church for renewing the life of the church today. This emphasis characterized much of his life and ministry, including his popular workshops, ecumenical endeavors, and many well-received books, including *The Divine Embrace, Ancient Future Worship, and Ancient Future Faith*. At the time of his death in 2007, he was the Myers Professor of Ministry at Northern Seminary in Lombard, Illinois. He also served as the founding president for the Institute for Worship Studies in Orange Park, Florida. In 2007, the Board of Trustees renamed the school the Robert E. Webber Institute for Worship Studies in honor of his vision and accomplishments. To carry on Webber's aspiration for Christian rejuvenation rooted in the consensus of the ancient church, Trinity School for Ministry in Ambridge, Pennsylvania, opened the Robert E. Webber Center for an Ancient Evangelical Future in 2012.

STEFANY WEBBER WELCH is the daughter of Robert E. Webber. She graduated from Wheaton College with a B.A. in English Literature. She is an avid reader and thinker. An aspiring yogini, she has recently completed a 200-hour yoga teacher training program. She lives in Grand Rapids, Michigan, with her husband, Tom, who helped shape the story in this book. Together they are raising four fantastic children.